THE FORTEAN TIMES BOOK OF

Life's Losers

THE FORTEAN TIMES BOOK OF

Life's Losers

COMPILED BY IAN SIMMONS
ILLUSTRATED BY GEOFF COUPLAND

JOHN BROWN PUBLISHING

First published in Great Britain in October 1996
by John Brown Publishing Ltd, The Boathouse,
Crabtree Lane, Fulham, London SW6 6LU, UK.
Tel 0171 470 2400. Fax 0171 381 3930.

ISBN 1-870870-816

Printed and bound in Great Britain
by BPC Paperbacks Ltd
A member of The British Printing Company Ltd

CONTENTS

INTRODUCTION

Luck is one of humanity's great obsessions. There cannot be a culture anywhere in the world without a concept of good and bad luck and a whole series of rituals, formal or informal to ensure that you get the right sort, and your enemies don't. Horoscopes claim to predict your future luck, gamblers believe they can get lucky and beat the odds to make a fortune, something which has become a major part of British life with the arrival of the National Lottery – it could be you, but you are 43 times more likely to die from falling out of bed than you are to win the jackpot.

It always seems that bad luck is more prevalent than good luck, but perhaps it is just that people talk about it more – maybe because it is more interesting. There is only really one kind of good luck, but bad luck comes in infinite variety. There is the usual kind of bad luck which underpins everyday life, giving us a malevolent background of stress, frustration and ambient misery, but there is also the special kind – the sort of bad luck above and beyond the call of duty that the Cosmic Joker must make special efforts to create, and it is that sort of bad luck that makes its way into the *Fortean Times* "Tough Shit" file.

Collected from newspapers the world over, a torrent of clippings comes through the letterbox of Fortean Towers and gets sorted into more than 30 categories. Some make it to the magazine, but there just isn't space for all of them. The ones collected here include classics that have appeared in *Fortean Times* over the years, plus many drawn from the vast backlog of wonderful "Tough Shit" tales we haven't previously had room for. I can't vouch for the absolute truth of every story, but what I can definitely say is that all have been printed as "fact" by newspapers, magazines and journals, and that the source for each one can be found in the references at the back, so you can make up your own mind about the more incredible.

It has been a total fascination to work through the piles of stories for this book. I joined the *FT* team as a result of my curiosity about the clippings that didn't make it to the mag, and this gave me a chance to wallow in them to my heart's content. I must extend my warmest thanks to the rest of the *FT* team for their advice and encouragement, and for drawing my attention to particularly juicy tales which I might otherwise have missed. Thanks are also due to the denizens of the Fortean mailing list on the Internet, for sending me stuff and for keeping my mind at the right pitch of surreality for the task, and most of all to my wife, Fiona, who lets me spend my life in the attic.

IAN SIMMONS

Why Bother?

Great efforts are supposed to bring great rewards – but it doesn't always work that way.

FRANK PERKINS of Los Angeles made an attempt on the world flagpole-sitting record in 1992. But after he came down he not only discovered he was eight hours short of the 400-day record, but also that his sponsor had gone bust, his girlfriend had left him, and his phone and electricity had been cut off.

A RAPTUROUS WELCOME awaited Antonio Gomez Bohorquez and Pascual Fuertes Noguera when they returned home to Murcia in southern Spain after pioneering a new route up Mount Sisha Pagma in the Himalayas. On studying specialist publications, however, they had to sheepishly admit that they had, in fact, climbed the wrong mountain.

IN CEBU CITY, Philippines, Enrique Quinanola made a

determined effort to kill himself. Quinanola, 21 and unemployed, attempted to hang himself, but relatives cut the rope and took him to hospital. While doctors prepared a sedative, he slipped away and ran to a nearby restaurant where he grabbed a knife and slashed his wrists. Police saw the incident and tried to subdue Quinanola, but he put up a terrific struggle, so the officers shot him, first in the leg, then in the chest. He died a few minutes later. His relatives sued the government for violating his civil liberties.

TIRING OF CROWDS attending football games at the Kennedy Stadium when the Washington Redskins were playing, Charles Buki moved from his home near the ground to Arlington, Virginia. He said parking was impossible on game days and he was sick of picking up beer bottles in his front yard. On arriving in Arlington he was "absolutely paralysed" to discover that his new home was only a short distance from the Redskins' planned new stadium. The *Washington Post* compared his fate to that of farmer Wilmer McLean, who fled Manassas, Virginia, after the American Civil War's first battle was fought there. He moved to Appomattox Courthouse, the eventual site of the final battle of the war, where Lee surrendered to Grant in McLean's living room.

ANOTHER WARTIME INCIDENT caused Danny Simpson of Ottawa, Canada, much grief. In 1990 he was given six years imprisonment for robbing a bank of $6000 using an elderly Colt .45-calibre pistol. He was arrested and the gun was impounded by the police, where it was recognised as an extremely rare collectors' item, worth between $12,000 and $100,000 dollars. It was made under licence by the Ross Rifle Company in Quebec City during WW1, one of only 100 Colt .45s ever made there. Simpson could have walked into any gun shop and sold the pistol for at least twice the haul from his raid without breaking the law.

ANOTHER ARMED ROBBER, jailed for eight years in Argentina, decided to hire a private detective to trace the father he had never met. The detective discovered the man's father was the warder of the prison in which he was incarcerated.

IAN LEWIS, 43, of Standish, Lancashire, was also interested in finding out about his family. He spent 30 years tracing his family tree back to the seventeenth century. He travelled all over Britain, talked to 2,000 relatives and planned to write a book about how his great-grandfather left to seek his fortune in Russia and how his grandfather was expelled after the Revolution. Then he found out he had been adopted when he was a month old and his real name was David Thornton. He resolved to start his family research all over again.

MARKKU TAHVAINEN drove his family 250 miles to a zoo in Finland in order to see the bears. When they returned home, though, they discovered footprints and droppings in their garden which revealed that in their absence they had been visited by a bear which had eaten their ducks.

AFTER THREE DAYS of uninterrupted heavy metal music from the flat next door, Gunthwilde Blom, 63, of Klagenfurt, Austria, began to get cross. She hammered on the walls and put notes under the door of the offending flat. All this had no effect so she confronted her neighbour, Wilma Kock, directly. Kock protested her innocence, but

Blom did not believe her, calling her a "venomous herring". When the noise continued Mrs Blom finally went berserk and pushed 20lbs of fresh herring through her neighbour's letter-box. Ms Kock called the police, who discovered while interviewing Blom that the music was actually coming from a radio she had inadvertently left on beneath her own bed. Unrepentant, she declared, "They didn't understand — Kock's a cow."

A SOUTH AFRICAN came six thousand miles to photograph the church clock in Grantchester, Cambridge, at ten to three, as in the Rupert Brooke poem. It had broken down and was stuck at 1.05.

Albin Birch's trek across the world had a similarly disappointing end. He set out for New Zealand from London to track down a cousin he had not seen for 30 years — but found a month-old corpse instead. Albin's 82-year-old cousin Bennett Birch was a recluse who lived in the remote settlement of Takehe in New Zealand's far north. He had died a month or so before Albin's arrival, but due to his reclusive habits no one had noticed.

Meanwhile, Martin Reeves travelled eight thousand miles to India to find parts for his 1957 Morris Cowley. His mission was successful, but when he got back to Brighton, he found the car had been stolen. Athlete John Oliver, 31, went all the way from Bournemouth, Dorset, to Nepal — a journey of over five thousand miles — to take part in his first marathon, only to sprain his ankle on the starting line.

SECURITY MEASURES bring their own headaches. In Broadway, Worcestershire, in 1990, a safe was unlocked for the first time since its key had been lost in 1942. All it contained was a note urging people not to lose the key. In

Mumbles, Swansea, Robin Branhall got tired of vandals who had broken the window of his surfing shop more than 20 times, so he fitted an unbreakable one. Arriving at his shop next day, he found the entire window had been stolen. Likewise, a Dutchman who invested more than £600 in a police-trained guard dog to protect his home in Schalkhar woke up two days later to find the house had been broken into. The only thing the burglars had taken was the dog.

A LONELY HEART who placed an ad in an unnamed Yorkshire newspaper seeking to meet a lady for outings and friendship received only one reply – from his mother. Had he had better luck, he would have been wise not to use the condoms issued by the New Zealand Health Department in their safe-sex guide. They were attached to the booklet by a staple through the middle.

LA CICCIOLINA, the Italian porno star MP, returned to her native Hungary in 1989 to visit the hamlet of Kiskunhalas in order to celebrate the departure of Soviet military forces from the land they had occupied since 1945. She marked the beginning of the withdrawal by releasing a white dove, but could only watch, along with bemused villagers, as the symbolic bird fluttered down onto a railway transporter's loading ramp and the first tank of the first regiment of the Soviet Southern Army Group 13th Division rolled right over it.

THE AVERAGE COST of rehabilitating a seal after the Exxon Valdez oil spill in Alaska was $80,000. Two of the most expensive of the animals were reintroduced to the wild at a special ceremony. Within two minutes they were both eaten by a killer whale.

SHEFFIELD CITY COUNCIL'S Norton Nurseries was home to a magnificent 25ft-tall succulent, *Agave americana*, which had survived WW2 and 50 British winters. In its native South America it normally flowers once every 15 years, but in the British climate that was believed to take 50–100 years. In 1988 it began to develop a flower spike and was excitedly tended by nurserymen awaiting the great event – until a council workman reversed his lorry over the plant, smashing it to oblivion.

A FIREMAN in Bath, using a metal detector to trace fire hydrants which had been covered with tarmac after road resurfacing, dug seven holes in the wrong places before realising that the device was being set off by the steel toe-caps of his boots.

WATER SUPPLIES also caused much vexation to historians trying to discover the identity of someone buried in the graveyard of Evercreech Church, near Shepton Mallet. They were trying to identify the person under a gravestone simply marked "H.W.P." until the Wessex Water Authority put them out of their misery by pointing out that it was simply a marker for the church's hot-water pipe.

IN 1996 Claude Arcens finally gave up his vigil under the Eiffel Tower. In 1984 someone on the tower dropped a purse which he found and kept, so he returned in the hope of retrieving other treasures. The only other thing he found during his 12-year wait was a lighter.

Mark of the Beast

Dogs are supposed to be man's best friend, but you wouldn't know it from looking at our files, which bulge with dog- and other animal-related disasters.

A RUSSIAN WOMAN who did nothing after her pitbull terrier savaged her husband got her come-uppance in spades. The beast turned on her and chewed off both her arms while she walked it in the park. The dog was shot.

SYLVESTER ATKINSON of Burnley denied any malice aforethought in the death of his neighbour, James Murray, 68. Furious when his dog, Scrappy, crapped on the kitchen floor, Atkinson grabbed the mutt and hurled him out of the back door. Unfortunately he hurled too hard and Scrappy soared over the garden fence to land on Mr Murray's head. Murray died of a heart attack bought on by the shock.

A 16-STONE MONGREL called Pugwash was the nemesis of his elderly one-legged owner who dozed off one afternoon, awoke, tried to get up and toppled over. The massive hound had grabbed his wooden leg and was chewing on it. The pensioner crawled towards the animal, who was still munching the leg. The dog wouldn't relinquish it so the man had to phone the RSPCA for help; but Pugwash prevented them from entering the flat and they eventually had to resort to pushing drugged meat through the letterbox to pacify him, after which he was found a new home and his owner a new leg.

IN LEIPZIG, a man who had his tongue cut off during a drunken row was unable to have it reattached. A cat had eaten it.

DOGS AND CARS can be a particularly hazardous combination, as Sherrif's Deputy Greg Chaney found out. He stopped a suspicious vehicle early one Sunday and ordered the occupants to get out and lie on the ground. His dog, Turbo, a German Shepherd, was sitting in the back seat, but to get a better view of the excitement he hopped into the front, bumping the car into gear as he did so. The car rolled forwards and onto 25-year-old Tracy Andrus, one of the prone suspects, trapping her beneath it.

66-year-old Dora Louise Wagners left her 1971 Oldsmobile in her drive with the motor running and her small black dog inside. This dog also managed to knock the car into gear, setting it moving, and as Mrs Wagners tried to climb into the rolling car she stumbled and was dragged more than 30 feet, ending up crushed to death between the vehicle and a log pile.

Incidents like this are not uncommon in the US where most cars have automatic transmissions, and dogs at the wheel account for several deaths a year.

SEVERAL PEOPLE each year also get shot by dogs. Farmer Franz Gilly met this fate in 1975 when his puppy jumped up and hit the trigger of the gun he was holding; and Petrus Roux of Villiersdorp near Capetown, South Africa, was seriously injured when driving a pick-up truck with his dog, Stompie, sitting on the front seat and a shotgun propped between them. The truck lurched, throwing Stompie off the seat and onto the gun, which blasted Roux with shotgun pellets at close range.

CALCULATED REVENGE or coincidence? Farmer Vincent Caroggio was shot by a rabbit. He was hunting them near Chartres, France, and after killing five he stopped for a rest, putting his shotgun down by his side. As he did so, another rabbit trod on the trigger, killing the farmer. In Sri Lanka, fisherman Anthony Fernando was also killed when his prey got the upper hand — a fork-tailed alligator garfish lept out of the sea and speared him to death. Nathon de Nascimento, fishing in the Amazon near Belem, was assassinated by an even more accurate fish. This one leapt out of the river and down his throat as he was having a good yawn, jamming too far in for anyone to reach its tail. He choked to death.

THE PREY has been known to exact its own price in other cases as well. In New Zealand a hunter loosed both barrels at a duck, missing it completely. The duck circled the hunter, then dived at him, hitting him in the face and breaking his glasses, his nose and a tooth.

Avian revenge can be posthumous too. While shooting grouse on Lord Bolton's estate at Wensley, near Leyburn, Yorkshire, Gilbert Fenwick got more than he bargained for when he bagged one bird. As he aimed for a second, the plummeting corpse smashed into his face, hurling him backwards into the heather unconscious and leaving him with a cut lip and two black eyes. "You wouldn't believe how painful a one-and-a-half-pound grouse is when it hits you at 60mph," he said afterwards. Emmanuelle Argand would: she was pregnant when she was thrown off a wall and into a 9ft ditch by a grouse impact during shooting on the Duke of Roxburghe's estate. Fortunately she did not lose the child, but was paralysed from the waist down by the accident. The case of Dutchman Anne Osinga has a tinge of "serves you right" about it. He had his cheekbone smashed by a plummeting 6lb goose, shot by one of his hunting companions. He was Chairman of the Friesian Society for the Protection of Birds at the time.

DOMESTIC ANIMALS can be just as vicious after death. Slaughterman Frank Harris had just killed a pig in a bacon factory in Lisemore, New South Wales, and was bending over the carcass when a muscular contraction threw one of the pig's legs in the air, striking the hand in which he was holding the knife and forcing the blade through his cheek.

ANIMAL LOVER Jose Quaritz of Cancun, Mexico, lavished attention on his pet frog, but was permanently blinded when the creature exploded in his face after overindulging in a feast of cat food.

FLIES ARE TROUBLESOME at the best of times, but they gave serious grief to Roberto Cazzola. He was out on his balcony in Milan, Italy, when a marauding fly provoked him into a fit of swatting which grew so wild that he toppled over the edge and crashed 50ft into the street below, breaking his arms, legs and three ribs.

OUR NEXT TALE has assumed urban-legend status, if it wasn't one to start with. Emilio Tarra, a crew-member for a yacht in the America's Cup race, was driving from Perth to Adelaide during the Australian leg of the 1986 competition when his car sideswiped a kangaroo and left it sprawled in the road. Assuming it was dead, Tarra dressed it in his Gucci blazer and propped it up against the car to take its photo. As he was focusing the camera, the beast, which was only stunned, came to its senses and, after smacking Tarra unconscious with its tail, bounded off into the bush still wearing the designer blazer, with his passport, $2000 and sixteen credit cards in its pockets.

ANOTHER STORY also has a faint scent of urban legend about it. An unnamed woman in Leipzig, it is claimed, wanted to emulate Cleopatra by bathing in ass's milk, so she stole a donkey. The plan went sour when the creature turned out to be male and brayed so loudly that neighbours called the police.

FIREMEN SPENT three hours rescuing a cow from the River Derwent in the spring of 1993. As they packed up to leave, it jumped back in again.

EDWARD AND ELIZABETH BRIMBLE were taking their Labrador-cross dog, Trudie, for her daily walk in Bungay, Suffolk, when she began to snarl and foam at the mouth. The Brimbles thought she was having a fit and pinned her down in the road for ten minutes as she howled, suffered convulsions and finally died. It was only when Mr Brimble gave her a farewell stroke and received an electric shock that he realised the ground was "live". Corroded wiring in a nearby lamp-post was sending a 240-volt current through the concrete. The Brimbles escaped because they were wearing rubber boots. If they hadn't held Trudie down she'd have escaped too.

FOR SOME YEARS, Blackpool Zoo has been trying to run a captive breeding programme for potaroos, a rabbit-sized Tasmanian marsupial. The species is "at risk" because males left together unsupervised have a tendency to tear each other's genitals off.

THE SOUTHERN RIDGE of Himlung Himal, a 23,387ft mountain in the Himalayas, had never been climbed when Berwyn Evans and three colleagues made the attempt in 1992. They failed, but not due to the usual reasons. They had stashed some of their supplies in advance to avoid having to carry heavy packs, but when they reached their depot they found it had been looted by giant birds which had made off with food, tents and even a gas cooker.

EVERY YEAR in the spring hordes of "twitchers", manic birdwatchers, descend upon the Scilly isles in the spring to catch sight of birds which are rarely seen in the British isles, but end up there having been blown off course while migrating. In 1993 an announcement by an expert twitcher on CB radio led to birdwatchers rushing to a small field to focus their binoculars on what they thought was a North American nighthawk. It turned out that the "sighting" was, in fact, a cowpat.

COWPATS, though, are not the most distressing things twitchers can find themselves watching. In October 1991 many converged on Pennington Marshes near Southampton to see a buff-breasted sandpiper from America. As they watched, a sparrowhawk dived down and killed it. On the same day in South Tyneside another sparrowhawk repeated the trick, offing a Siberian yellow-browed warbler as it fed on insects in a garden in Whitburn. In Ireland, the first American bittern recorded in the British Isles for eight years made it across the Atlantic to County Wexford in 1990, and ended up in the jaws of Mick Reville's dog. At Slimbridge Wildfowl and Wetlands Trust in Gloucestershire, a rare grey-cheeked thrush turned up after having been blown off course on its migration from Canada to South America. It announced its arrival by smacking into the glass door at the Trust's office, breaking its neck.

PAUL CORNEY was driving along a country road near Portsmouth in 1989 when suddenly there was a cloud of feathers and a burst of steam as a bird of some sort smashed into his radiator. He got out to find the remains of a strik-ing-looking duck embedded in his grille, but he was not knowledgeable enough to recognise a rare UK visitor, the red-crested pochard. The pack of angry-looking people charging up the road towards him were, though: they were birdwatchers who had spent several days and nights in the reeds waiting for a glimpse of the bird. Paul didn't hang round to make excuses. "I legged it!" he said.

A RARE Cabot's tragopan was recognised on a poultry stall in a Hong Kong market where it was about to be made into soup. It was rescued and taken to the colony's zoo, where it promptly died of pneumonia. The Rufous fishing owl, however, was not so lucky in escaping the pot. British ornithologist Phillip Ball trekked into the Nigerian hinterland to see the bird, one of the rarest owls in existence, when he heard one had been seen in the Edo region. On arriving after a hazardous journey, the tribe with which he was staying laid on a sumptuous feast, with a delicious stew as the main course. After four helpings Ball asked what it was and the chief flapped his arms and made hooting sounds. Realizing that he'd just eaten the object of his quest, Ball took some photos of hippos and returned home.

STAFF AT QINGDAO ZOO, China, had gathered to celebrate the birth of the first baby walrus born in a Chinese zoo. As they watched, its 40-stone mother rolled over and squashed it. A similar fate has been suffered by 200 female sea-lions in a cove near San Miguel Island, off the California coast. At first local fishermen were suspected of shooting them, but then a national Marine Fisheries biologist, Robert DeLong, spotted a massive bull sea-lion mating with a female. She was gasping and suffocated within a minute. The bull is a hybrid between a Californian sea-lion and a Stellar's sea-lion, and weighs almost twice what a normal male sea-lion does, eight times the weight of an adult female.

PUGNACIOUS the cat also ended up feeling crushed after getting stuck on a ledge outside his owner Marjorie Daley's ninth-floor flat in Sydney, Australia. Mrs Daley called to him to come in but the cat was too scared to move, so she climbed onto the railings to reach out to him. As she did so, she lost her balance and fell forward, knocking Pugnacious off the ledge. They both hurtled earthwards, but miraculously a skip full of rotten pumpkins broke their fall. Pugnacious hit the skip fractionally before his owner, who landed on top of him, crushing him to death.

CHAPTER THREE

Asking For It

**It takes no great skill to work out
that some ventures are likely to end
in tears, but that doesn't stop
people embarking on them.**

A CANADIAN WOMAN who claimed to have X-ray
vision attempted to prove it by driving blindfold down a city
street. Lauren Rhoda, 27, made the attempt in Ottawa, running over a pedestrian and breaking his toe, then knocking
down a lamp and ploughing into three cars, one a police
vehicle, before she gave up. She was fined £400 and banned
from driving for two years.

THE RAT TRAP, a police anti-theft car, caught 31 thieves
in 18 months in Newcastle upon Tyne. It was left inviting-
ly around the streets for people to steal, but was designed
with doors that automatically locked and windows which
could not be opened from the inside, trapping thieves until
the police arrived. To complete the job, the Ford Sierra also
had an engine which died after only driving 20 yards. Or at

least that was what it was supposed to do. In October 1992 it was driven off without trace from Bath Lane in the city. "There was a malfunction," a rather tight-lipped police spokesman said. Equally ineffective as an anti-crime measure was a life-size cardboard cut-out policeman which stood in Morrison's supermarket in Ripon, North Yorkshire. It too was stolen.

NEEDLESS TO SAY, fooling around with dangerous animals is never a good idea, as Jordan Lazelle of Hayling Island in Hampshire found out. Jordan, 19, was the proud owner of Twiggy, a scorpion, and one evening, on returning from the pub, he decided to express his affection by kissing the beast goodnight. His love was not reciprocated, and Twiggy stung him on the tongue, requiring him to be rushed to hospital.

In Terney, in the far east of Russia, a hunter with a longing for a foreign car set out to shoot a tiger so he could sell the skin to pay for the vehicle. He was even less lucky than Lazelle: the tiger not only bit him, it ate him alive.

LARRY COLLINS, a handyman at the Benedict Bird Ranch in Sacremento, California, claimed to have been kicked and trampled by an ostrich-like creature while putting up a sign. The owners said the claim was ridiculous. The sign Collins was attempting to fix warned of dangerous birds.

OVER THE CENTURIES many have suffered for their religion, but Parson Ezra Piner of Johannesburg might have chosen his sermon more wisely the day twins Gina and Paulina Weams were in his congregation. The Weamses, each of them over 20 stones in weight, sat through Piner's searing sermon about the laziness of fat people, then battered him senseless, breaking his nose.

SIMILARLY, walking about with a placard reading "The End is Nigh" might be seen as encouraging fulfilment of the prophecy. It certainly was for one doomsayer in Barcelona: as he carried his placard across a busy road in the city he was knocked down and killed.

WEDDING NIGHT JOKES are also best avoided as they have a nasty habit of backfiring. Such was the case with an unnamed bride in New York, who bought a replica chastity belt so that she could wind up her new husband by locking it and pretending to lose the key. She locked it all right, but then the key really did vanish, somewhat attenuating the night's traditional activity. "I think the best man knew something about it," opined a friend.

ANOTHER FOREDOOMED activity was Gabrielle Schmitt's psychology degree project. She rented a room in her flat to carpenter Andi Weber in order, unbeknownst to him, that she could nag him day and night to study his reactions. He reacted all right: after weeks of unrelenting needling he finally snapped and laid into Gabrielle with an axe, hitting her over the head with it four times. Gabrielle is now mentally handicapped, but Andi was given a lenient jail sentence of four years and three months because he was provoked.

JIAN JUN XI, an art student at Goldsmiths College in London created an exhibit for his end-of-term show which was, he said, "Trying to give a new definition of money." He drew his life savings of £1225.69 out of the bank and scattered it over the gallery floor. On collecting the cash up after the exhibition closed, he found that £40 had gone for a walk during the show. Also on the sticky end of a money scam was Terry Offord, boss of a company which sells machines for detecting forged banknotes. He sold two of them and was paid in fake £50 notes.

A DELEGATE to the 1991 World Conference on Memory was forced to ring organisers at Lancaster university after he forgot which days he had booked to attend. A similar embarrassing lapse afflicted Tom Morton, who has instant recall of over 20,000 phone numbers, decks of cards and all Olympic medal winners for the past century. He forgot which day he was due to appear on Granada TV to demonstrate his skills, and turned up a week early.

Entirely in character, though, was Tony Randall's non-appearance on the TV show *Wake Up America* as a spokesman for National Sleep Disorder Month – he had overslept and missed his guest spot.

NEWSAGENT Dennis Brightey of Brandon, Suffolk, pinned up a "No milk today" sign. Seconds later, milkman David Roberts lost control of his float after swerving to miss a car and crashed into the shop with 1,000 pints on board.

IN THE SOVIET UNION one of the country's vast band of faith healers felt ready for the ultimate test of his powers. When E. Frenkel stepped in front of a goods train outside the city of Astrakhan he left a note reading: "First I stopped a bicycle, cars and a streetcar, now I'm going to stop a train". The train driver saw him walking beside the track a long way ahead, but as he approached Frenkel dropped his briefcase and stepped onto the tracks with his arms raised, head lowered and body tensed. The report records: "Emergency braking didn't help – a tragedy occurred."

WHILE MAKING A FILM about the importance of wearing a seat-belt, Anthony Galati suffered serious head injuries after losing control of his car in Los Angeles. He was not wearing a seat-belt.

ANOTHER FEAT whose fate could perhaps have been easily foreseen was Salvator Bontempi's attempt to catch a bowling ball dropped from a 12-storey building for a bet. A friend dropped the ball, but Bontempi missed and the hurtling 16lb ball smashed into his foot, breaking every bone in it. Similarly, Aurelio Capuzzo should have figured out that William Tell re-enactments are not a brilliant idea, especially when you are both the marksman and the target. He attempted to shoot an apple off his own head, live on Italian television, using a remote-controlled crossbow — and missed, hitting himself in the eye with the arrow instead. Our source does not say whether he survived his *faux pas*.

FRED TURNER set out from Beaufort, South Carolina, on a cross-country walk to reassure himself that "99 per cent of the people in the world are generally good". He had only travelled 35 miles when the other one per cent caught up with him. Two men in a rusty pick-up truck accosted him and asked if he was the guy walking across the country. He said yes, they demanded his wallet and threw him off a bridge into the Savannah River on the Georgia State line. Turner survived the 75-foot drop and floated a mile and a half to an island where he spent the night. He was rescued by fishermen the next day. He had a black eye, wrenched back, turned ankle and twisted knee, but planned to hit the road again soon. His optimism was undimmed, he said. A similar fate was suffered by a priest in 1986. He was travelling on the New York subway reading a book titled *When*

Bad Things Happen to Good People when he was mugged by two transvestites.

THE GOOD INTENTIONS of Chris P. Carrot were also thwarted when he launched his campaign against animal cruelty dressed as a 7ft carrot. When he visited a Texas school the headmaster used him as an example of why the children should never talk to strangers.

A SUSPICIOUS-LOOKING cardboard box was found outside a Territorial Army centre in Bristol in 1993. The TA called the police, who in turn called an Army bomb-disposal unit who blew up the box — to find it full of leaflets on how to deal with suspicious-looking packages.

U-BOAT COMMANDER Wolfgang Luth met his end during the Second World War when he gave strict instructions to guards to shoot anyone who did not give the right password. One day he forgot the password and a sentry shot him dead

Damned If You Do...

"Between the Devil and the deep blue sea"; "Out of the frying pan and into the fire"... Double jeopardy is familiar to everyone. But some people get tougher breaks than others.

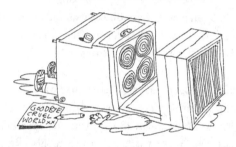

THIS ONE HAD TO HAPPEN sooner or later! On 10 August 1994, Malcolm and Sue Burt decided to visit Longleat Safari Park in their Renault 25. They got as far as the tiger enclosure before the car caught fire. They would have had the unpalatable choice of sitting tight and burning, or getting out and facing the tigers, had the flames not shorted out the electronic locking system, trapping them in the car. Fortunately Warden John Mizen managed to drive the circling tigers away just as the Burts forced the driver's door open, enabling them to leap into his patrol car. Clearly the Cosmic Joker is a believer in the principle of "if it's worth doing once, it's worth doing twice", as almost a year to the day later, on 7 August 1995, Steven and Jane Marshall were sitting in another Renault, this time an Espace, in another tiger enclosure, this time at Windsor

Safari Park, when their engine also caught fire. The Marshalls, along with their two children and Mrs Marshall's mother were rescued by rangers who positioned Land Rovers on either side of the car to keep nine tigers away.

KURT LINDBERG also survived his flaming fate, but only just. Having accidentally set his couch on fire, he rushed next door to get a fire extinguisher and broke in through a side window, thinking his neighbour Bjorn Edlund was out. He was wrong. Bjorn was in and, thinking Kurt was a burglar, shot him. Fortunately Lindberg was only wounded and recovered in hospital. Discovering his mistake, Edlund redeemed himself by putting the fire out.

FIRES SEEM to lead to this sort of situation. Ioannis Philippou, 50 from Cyprus, was huddling over a paraffin heater, trying to keep warm during freezing weather, when he accidentally overturned it, setting fire to his clothes. Mr. Philippou rushed outside and hurled himself into a shallow reservoir, dousing the flames but drowning in the process.

WASPS WERE ADAM ZEBRAK'S DOWNFALL. He was at an auction in Sussex when one flew up his shirt, making him flail wildly in an attempt to swat it. The auctioneer interpreted Zebrak's wild movements as bids for an antique cigarette lighter, pushing the price up to £500, and he was forced to buy it. David Martin of Retford, Nottinghamshire, also had wasp trouble. While walking his dog he had to jump into the River Idle to avoid being attacked by a swarm. He was bitten on the leg by a pike instead.

POLICE escorted Richard Swearingin (can that really be his name?) to hospital at high speed after he discovered his baby daughter was choking to death. But once one-year-old Amy had been successfully treated, Wisconsin police booked him for breaking the speed limit on his life-saving journey.

IN ZIMBABWE in 1994, a woman arrested for shoplifting stripped before police to prove she had not stolen clothes. The shoplifting charges were dropped but she was booked for indecent exposure instead.

MIRACLES may not be all they are made out to be, as Joseph Charpentier found out to his cost after his 16th visit to Lourdes in 1988. Once a quadriplegic, earlier visits to the shrine had returned the use of his hands, and after this one he was able to leave his wheelchair outside the Lourdes grotto. As required by religious tradition, Charpentier told the world about his miracle cure. Unfortunately this included social security officials, who reasoned that as he was no longer disabled, he no longer warranted his monthly 8,000 franc (£944) invalidity pension. They cancelled it, leaving him to survive on his 5,000 franc electrician's pension.

A MOTORIST who crashed at Elm, Cambridge, escaped the accident unharmed, but returning to his car after phoning emergency services, he brushed against an 11,000 volt cable dangling from a pylon bent in the accident and was instantly electrocuted. Vittoria Luise suffered a similar fate when a fierce gust of wind blew his bubble car into the River Sele near Naples. He managed to break a window, clamber out and swim ashore, but when he got there a tree blew down and killed him.

GEORGE SMITH, aged 86 and in poor health, decided to end it all by gassing himself in his oven. But before he could complete the task, fate took a hand. As he prepared, the top-heavy gas stove toppled over and crushed him to death. Although he left a suicide note, the coroner ruled it was an accidental death.

A WOMAN DRIVER who had her bag snatched while she waited at traffic lights gave chase to the thieves in her Mercedes. The thieves dropped the bag, but when she got out to retrieve it they stole the car instead.

OBSTETRICIAN Dr Linda R. Goudy cancelled a Caribbean cruise after a premonitory dream convinced her that if she went she would die in her car. Four days later, on 4 October 1993, she was found strangled in her Saab in the parking lot of the hospital where she worked in Stoneham, Massachusetts.

A FLORIDA MAN was rushed to hospital after a snake bit him on the finger. Doctors removed the poison, saved the finger, and told him to stick it in an icepack. Two weeks later the finger had to be amputated due to frostbite. Snakes were no help to Shahidul Islam, a snake-charmer from Bangladesh, either. He was on a bus which plunged off the road and was one of the three people who died when his escaped snakes prevented rescuers reaching the 30 injured.

A FARMER aged 54 climbed five flights of stairs in a hospital in Messina, Sicily, to have a heart check-up. When he reached the top he collapsed and died of a massive coronary.

Not Their Day

Some days you wish you'd stayed in bed, but take comfort. No matter how bad those days may seem, there's always someone having a worse one.

WEATHERMAN Michael Fish will always be remembered for assuring the UK that there was no hurricane on the way the day before the country was devastated by one in 1987, but he's got a long way to go before he catches up with his Indian colleague, Cibonco Mala. When Cibonco forecast sun, it snowed, while his warning of frost heralded a heatwave. TV chiefs pulled the plug on his New Delhi show when he began crying on air. He went into hiding following death threats.

AN ISRAELI WOMAN, according to the Jerusalem Post in 1988, found a cockroach in her house, stamped on it, threw it in the lavatory and sprayed a full can of insecticide after it when it refused to die. Coming home from work, her husband sat on the toilet, smoked a cigarette and dropped the butt into the bowl when he finished, igniting the insecticide fumes and "seriously burning his sensitive parts". Two ambulance men, shaking with laughter at the incident, dropped the man's stretcher down the stairs, which broke his pelvis and some ribs. The newspaper later retracted the story saying it could not substantiate the report, which is not surprising as it seems to be an urban legend, appearing in some form or another since at least the Second World War.

CONSTABLE MALCOLM HODGESON helped arrest three Scotsmen in South Yorkshire, suspected of car theft and other crimes. In January 1990 he had to make the 616-mile return trip to Kirkcaldy, Fife, to give evidence at their trial, only to be told the case had been adjourned. He wrote to the court giving his holiday dates in the hope of avoiding a clash, but was told as he prepared to leave for the Swiss Alps that he would have to attend court in the middle of his break. Hodgeson borrowed £450 and flew to Scotland, where he was told the case had been adjourned again. This time, however, he was allowed to give his evidence at a special sitting. He flew back to Switzerland to discover that his luggage had ended up in Hamburg, where a German anti-terrorist squad had mistaken it for a bomb and blown it up.

DIY is an activity fraught with hazards, but this did not daunt a Mr Drew of Dartford. While attempting to renew a shower curtain he fell off his ladder, splintering the bath panel while his falling hammer cracked the bath and his drill smashed the washbasin. He abandoned the shower and went downstairs to repair a fireplace, but gave that up too when he poked his hammer through the TV screen. With great perseverance he took his ladder outdoors to paint the bath-room window – and fell off again. This time his chisel smashed through the window itself and finished the devastation of the bathroom by cracking the lavatory bowl, while Mr Drew himself went through the carport roof.

A SEEMINGLY LESS HAZARDOUS PASTIME is fishing, but Staffordshire milkman Steve Carte would not agree. He went fishing on the River Teme in 1995, but on arrival found all the best spaces gone, along with his bait, which had disappeared between his home in Tamworth and the riverbank. He rushed to Worcester for some more, picking up a £15 ticket for parking on double yellow lines. Finally on the riverbank, he fished fruitlessly for nine hours, then, just as he was about to pack up he got a bite. As he reeled it in, he stepped on his spare rod (worth £100) and broke it into three pieces, then lost the nine-pound barbel as he landed it. His car had a flat tyre by then, and he gashed his hand on a wall as he went to the pub for a pint. When he got home he locked his keys in the car and had to wait on the doorstep for several hours until his wife came home.

MOTORCYCLIST Gyula Andratti was waiting for the barriers to go up at a country level-crossing in Hungary when a horse and cart drew up behind him, followed by an elegant sports car. The roar of the train startled the horse, which reared and bit Gyula on the arm. He punched it on the nose. The horse shied, smashing the cart into the car. The farmer got down to try and pacify the other two men, tethering his goat to the crossing barrier. The barrier then went up, lifting the goat and hanging it from its rope.

THE COMBINATION of cars and animals was also pretty disastrous for Al Fitzwalter. As he got into his car, a snake hiding in it bit him on the left leg. Trying to stamp on the snake, Fitzwalter hit the accelerator, making the car rocket into the garage where it knocked over a petrol can which caught fire, burning both garage and house to the ground. Al has only one leg, having lost his right one in Vietnam. His claim for compensation failed, leaving him penniless, and his wife left him. Then came the accident. "I thought, I've only got one leg and a snake's biting it," said Al.

MORE AUTOMOTIVE HORRORS were suffered by Tony Middlehurst, editor of *Top Car* magazine, which reports on souped-up hatchbacks. On Saturday 14 August 1993, the back door of his Vauxhall Cavalier burst open, scraping along a wall. Two days later, as he hurtled down the M2, bolts fell from an overhead bridge, cracking the windscreen and wrecking the bonnet. On the Tuesday the Cavalier was finally written off in a collision with a juggernaut and two test cars which Middlehurst was driving exploded. On Wednesday, he switched to a Citroen and suffered a run-in with a van on a narrow street, then on Thursday his replacement Vauxhall had its front end stoved in in an encounter with another van on a South London roundabout. "It all started when someone gave me some lucky crystals," Middlehurst said. "I've thrown them away." His next car was sprinkled with holy water.

AIRCRAFT rather than cars were the nemesis of Humphrey Cain, President of the Folklore Society of Australia, when he visited Wangaratta airport to open a vintage aircraft exhibition. When he made his speech he found he could not be heard above the roar of the engine of a Dragweave Triplane which had its engine jammed on. As he was moved to a "quiet corner" a microlite took off and crashed into the ladder he was meant to speak from. Finally, as he made his way back to the refreshment tent, Mrs Margaret McCracken, an 83-year-old amateur parachutist, landed on his head.

IN 1994 a 29-year-old woman was chosen as the subject of a research project into the psychology of good and bad luck at Hertfordshire University. She has suffered a string of bereavements, broken bones and house fires and during one 50-mile journey had eight car accidents.

LONELY Peter Ditert tried to commit suicide by throwing himself in front of a car, but only succeeded in knocking himself out, so he tried again, this time plunging a hair-dryer into his bath. It blew a fuse. Next, he slashed his wrists, but not deep enough, so he went on to swallow rat poison, which he promptly threw up. After this, he filled his house with gas, but nothing happened; tried to shoot himself with a home-made pistol, which jammed; drove off an embankment at 70mph, escaping with cuts and bruises; drank brake fluid, which he puked again; took sleeping pills and was found and rushed to hospital; then finally drove crazily down a busy street crashing into 14 cars, getting only a headache and 14 angry drivers on his case for his pains.

A SIMILAR TACTIC was also the last resort of Huang Chia-Yuan, a failed novelist from Taipei. He was depressed by repeated rejections of his work, so purchased a copy of a Japanese volume entitled *The Complete Suicide Manual* and tried to put it into practice. He first tried hara-kiri, but used a potato peeler which broke against his ribs; next it was wet fingers in a live light socket, but while wearing rubber-soled shoes; and so on, up to the overdose. However, as his pills turned out to be indigestion tablets, he resorted to smashing up luxury cars with a hammer in the hope their owners might kill him. Huang was nearly right too: a crazed Lexus owner was dangling him head-first over a street vendor's deep-frying wok when police finally caught up with him.

ABEL RUIZ tried to make his appointment with destiny in front of the Gerona-Madrid express after being jilted. However, he fell between the rails and suffered only minor injuries, so after first-aid at Gerona hospital he stepped in front of a lorry, again only receiving slight injuries. Back inside he promised doctors he wouldn't try again. Nonetheless, an hour later he was back on a stretcher. He had been trampled by a runaway horse — a complete accident. This time his injuries were serious, but he pulled through and said he was "glad to be alive".

DOMINIQUE GUIHOLT was also glad to be alive after she survived a 3,700-foot drop when her parachute failed to open and she miraculously landed in bales of hay in a field. The feeling didn't last long: four hours later she slipped on her bathroom floor and smashed her skull on the toilet, dying instantly. It seems if you gotta go, you gotta go!

YOUR WEDDING is supposed to be the happiest day of your life, and so is inevitably the focus for all manner of horrors. However, few find the event as fraught as Paul McLean did in 1994. When he went to the church to check his wedding plans he found it had collapsed, so he sought out the priest, only to find he'd had a nervous breakdown. Checking on his reception venue in Los Angeles, he discovered that it had burnt down, and then found out his bridal home had no electricity or water. His jinx started the day he proposed to his girlfriend Denise at home in Colchester, Essex. He flew her to Paris to actually pop the question on top of the Eiffel Tower, but she was afraid of heights and fainted. Undeterred, Paul dropped to his knees at ground level, only to realise the ring was still on the tour coach, which had forgotten to pick them up.

KIRK WILSON'S WEDDING to Sara Manners was possibly even more traumatic. On Sara's hen night, her mother's camera developed a fault and none of the pictures came out. On the morning of the wedding, in Brundall, Norfolk, Jonathan Manners, the bride's brother and chief usher, fainted in the heat and had to be supported throughout the ceremony by his mother. At the reception the icing on the wedding cake melted and the top tier collapsed, falling upside down on the floor. When the bride arrived at the honeymoon suite in a Norwich hotel, the roses in her bouquet triggered an asthma attack. She discovered she had not packed an inhaler, so at 3am she was rushed to hospital with her husband holding an oxygen bottle, but recovered in time to breakfast at the hotel. Later that morning, the groom's brother, James Wilson, drove the newlyweds to Stanstead airport for their flight to the Canary Islands. His car caught fire as he pulled into the airport car-park and they had to douse the flames with cans of cold drink. Meanwhile the wedding video, still inside the camcorder, had been stolen in a burglary at a friend's house in Blofield.

AFTER WORKING IN SAUDI ARABIA for 10 years, Narciso Dapat returned to the Phillipines. On arrival he discovered his luggage had been lost, and as he left the airport he was robbed of the money he'd saved from his overseas job. With his remaining cash he went to a bar, where, after getting thoroughly blotto drowning his sorrows, he began chasing people with a club. With a mob after him, he ducked into a nearby house where, arming himself with a kitchen knife, he took an 11-year-old boy hostage. Following an 11-hour drama which ended at Manila airport where he tried to catch a plane to his home province of Capiz, he was finally arrested. The boy's parents, touched by Mr Dapat's misfortune, decided not to press charges.

FOUR SRI LANKAN servicemen were taking part in a military exercise in a 10ft open boat when a cyclone pushed them out to sea. They drifted for 43 days, crossing the Bay of Bengal and the Andaman Sea, finally washing ashore on the coast of Thailand — where they were arrested and thrown in gaol for entering the country without papers.

TO FINISH WITH, a classic tale from 1839. A boy from Gideon Hunt, near Allentown in Pennsylvania, fell into his father's millpond while sliding on the ice. One of his brothers fell in trying to rescue him. A third and fourth brother, then the father also went through the ice. The father and one boy managed to climb out, but the rest were drowned. At the funeral of the boys, the horses pulling one of the carriages became restive, dashing the vehicle to pieces, and the uncle who owned it had his collar bone broken or dislocated. Those who had been in the carriage got into another, which was also overturned and broken. The horses then ran against the carriage of another uncle, upsetting it and throwing the occupants out of it. When the father returned from the funeral, he found his house was on fire.

Dead Unlucky

The ultimate doom which awaits us all comes at the hand of the Grim Reaper, but some of us check out on a particularly doomed note, and for a few, bad luck continues beyond the grave.

SALVATORE CHIRILINO reached for a lucky four-leaf clover on a clifftop in Vibo Marina, Italy, and plunged 150 feet to his death. His wife said, "He slipped on the wet grass and went over the side." A police spokesman helpfully added, "It's just not lucky for everyone."

THE NAKED BODIES of an 18-year-old secretary and her 55-year-old accountant boss were discovered in their office toilet where they had died during a sex session. The man's horrified wife made the find when she went looking for him after he failed to come home. Police in Madrid believe they were killed by gas from a faulty water heater.

RETIRED COAL MERCHANT Peter Evans of West Kirby, Merseyside, bought a new £35,000 cottage in

Hertfordshire, but died before telling his family where it was. His sister, Aileen Hearn, 67, appealed to local estate agents to help her find it. "The house must now be empty and he had dogs which must be somewhere," she said.

THE HUSBAND AND THREE SONS of Austrian housewife Aloisia Ruckenstuhl were killed in four separate accidents, all within 20 yards of each other. The tragedies all happened in the village of Mitteraich where the main road runs beside the railway line, near a tombstone-shaped marker reading "4.5 Kilometres". The first to die was Aloisia's 19-year-old son Peter, who was killed by a car near the spot in 1975. Six months later Josef Jr, was hit by a train as he crossed the tracks on his moped, again near the marker. In 1979, after attending a concert in town with her husband Josef, she left him talking to friends. On the way home her husband was struck and killed by a train near the fateful spot. Aloisia said, "My world fell apart, now there is only my nine-year-old son Walter left." One year later, while tobogganing Walter hit a lamp-post near the 4.5 kilometre marker, ruptured his spleen and died in hospital.

VANCOUVER GENERAL HOSPITAL apologised to a murder victim's relatives after they had filed past the man's open coffin to discover his killer's corpse in it, wearing the suit they'd bought. The hospital had released the wrong corpse to the funeral home. How the murderer and his victim ended up as corpses in the same hospital is not explained.

AN UNDERTAKER drove 560 miles to a funeral before realising he had left the body behind. He was driving the hearse from the West German town of Bottrop to Zagreb,

Croatia, but a colleague pointed out the oversight in a telephone conversation at the German-Austrian border.

FUNERAL ATTENDANTS visiting the Bridge View Nursing home in Whitestone, Queens, New York, left the body behind, but carried away the deceased's sleeping roommate in a body bag instead. Fortunately signs of life were noticed as the "body" was prepared for embalming, and the woman recovered in hospital.

NONE OF HAMID AFIFI'S four children wanted to be responsible for the 72-year-old man's upkeep, so they entombed him alive in their family vault in Cairo, where he remained for 45 days until rescued by gravediggers. He caused a panic when he returned to his house, as his children thought it was his ghost returning to haunt them.

Julia Carson's return from the dead had a more dramatic effect. When she sat up in her coffin in a New York funeral parlour and asked what was going on, the shock was so great that her daughter dropped dead on the spot.

A SAILOR'S request for burial at sea caused a major security alert at Faslane nuclear submarine base on the Clyde. Delivered to the base unannounced, security guards found the package suspicious and called in a bomb disposal squad who subjected it to a controlled explosion. Fortunately the urn containing the man's ashes was not destroyed, and they were later committed to the sea from the submarine on which he had served. A Navy spokeswoman said, "This was a very regrettable incident."

SMOKER JUNE TAYLOR made her final attempt to give up smoking in 1986 and, as on every previous occasion, she suffered the violent withdrawal symptoms which had always led to her starting up again. This time she did not have that option. Eight hours after her last puff, the withdrawal symptoms became so extreme that she suffered a massive asthma attack which killed her.

ROMEO AND JULIET has been re-enacted in a modern setting on more than one occasion. Ralph Claridge, 29, jumped to his death from his tenth-floor flat in Mitcham, Surrey, when he found his wife, Janice, had taken an overdose. Within minutes she regained consciousness, but unlike Juliet, she refrained from killing herself.

A TRICK which brought about a wife's death was played by Tom Hansen, who placed a pile of plastic vomit on his wife Kirsten's expensive new carpet. On seeing the fake sick she was so horrified that she had a massive heart-attack and died on the spot.

ALTONA BROWN, aged 90, had bought a coffin for $2,946, in preparation for the inevitable. Brown, who lived in a nursing home in Fairbanks, Alaska, was receiving Social Security income and Medic-aid benefits. Government officials declared the coffin was an asset, and said that until she sold it they would cut off her benefits.

IN DRAPERSTOWN in Ireland, Charlie Rogers, 67, was helping to dig the grave of his brother Patrick. When the grave was complete, Charlie helped the gravedigger out of the hole, steadying himself on the heavy marble memorial which marked the family grave. As he did so, the soft soil gave way and the three-quarters-of-a-ton stone came crashing down on top of him, crushing him to death.

CHAPTER SEVEN

Wrath of God

It is said that those whom the gods notice they destroy, so perhaps it is not surprising that worshippers of all varieties seem to get more stick than average from the fickle finger of fate.

A TEENAGER expected to die after falling from a 10th-floor window made an excellent recovery over a six-week period. He had been resucitated, put on a life-support machine, received seven times his normal blood volume in transfusions and had multiple fractures of the skull, spine, pelvis, knee and leg repaired. Then suddenly he plunged into dangerous decline, suffering from persistent blood poisoning. Intensive investigation to find the source of the infection finally tracked it down to holy water that his aunt from Ireland was liberally sprinkling over him during her daily visits. The water, which was just tap water blessed by a priest, mixed with some from Lourdes and other holy places, was found to contain precisely the same strain of bacterium responsible for the poisoning which had nearly killed the boy a second time.

THE PROTESTANT TRUTH SOCIETY publishes an informative little pamphlet entitled "Papal Blessings and Curses" which records information about those unfortunate people who have suffered grim fates after receiving a Papal blessing, and others who have continued to thrive after a pontifical cursing. Those who have come to a sticky end include the Crown Princess of Brazil whose baby was born hideously deformed after she was blessed by the Pope. She later died in exile, as did the Emperor of Mexico's widow, also blessed, who had by then become "a hopeless maniac" as well.

In 1870 the Pope blessed a steamer full of nuns heading for South America, which sank *en route,* drowning everyone aboard. A subsequent Pope gave the *Italia* airship a cross to place at the North Pole. It never made it: the airship foundered, broke in two and half the crew were killed. More recently, another source recorded how a new Roman Catholic church in Belfast, including a foundation stone blessed by the Pope, was destroyed by a bomb shortly after it opened.

DOOMSDAY CULT LEADER Gerhard Wolff killed himself after his wife scribbled "666" on his forehead while he slept. When he woke he saw the sign of the devil in the mirror and hanged himself. Wolff, 58, from Dresden in Germany left a note reading, "The Devil has me in his grip. There is no escape."

DUBLIN PRIEST Sean O'Leary urged his choir to put more effort into singing "I Wonder Where I'm Bound" by jumping up and down. He soon found out where he was bound: the iron grid he was standing on collapsed and he disappeared into a heating duct.

THE BRIXTON ACTION STATION theatre company attempted to stage a play called "CruciFiction" during 1986. This was an iconoclastic look at the Easter story, replacing legend with rational explanation, albeit somewhat sensationalised. However, the production did not prosper. The first Jesus was knocked off his bike by a lorry on the way to rehearsals and broke his leg, then his replacement slipped on an icy pavement and broke his arm. Judas dropped out to take care of his father after a suicide attempt, then Peter, James and John quit after a disagreement with the director. Deciding the play was cursed, the rest of the cast left while the going was good.

With nine days to go the play was totally recast, but even this did not stem the tide of disaster. The latest Jesus, accompanied by Mary Magdalene, walked out after twenty pages of the script read-through when they discovered Jesus was portrayed as a wino. This triggered the director's long-overdue nervous breakdown, leaving the company with no choice but to cancel the whole show.

GOSPEL PREACHER PAUL WREN decided to demonstrate the might of the almighty by picking up a member of the congregation with his teeth. " I do this to make you realise how the Lord can give you great strength and how uplifting He can be" he explained before leaning over the pulpit to pick up 27-stone Joe Pearce in a harness which he gripped in his teeth. As he strained to make the lift, Pearce remained firmly earthbound until, finally, the effort wrenched out five of the preacher's front teeth. He bravely mumbled his way through a 30-minute sermon no one could understand before heading for a dentist in Carbondale, Illinois. When he could speak clearly again he reflected, "I'll have to find a new way to prove the power of the Lord."

91-YEAR-OLD ADELAIDE DOUGLAS of Queensland, Australia ordered a religious statue through the mail from AVA Enterprises, but instead of the Virgin Mary statuette she was expecting, she was sent a fearsome looking nine-inch dildo and a sex manual. A spokesman for the company, Darryl Christmas, apologised, explaining that the company dealt in both religious trinkets and sex aids, and that mix-ups occasionally occurred.

IN YUMA, ARIZONA, elders of the 1,000-strong Smoke Red Indian tribe were so concerned about the lengthy drought they were suffering that they gathered the tribe's young warriors together to perform their ancient raindance. Within four hours of the ceremony beginning, torrential rains had flooded their reservation, knocking down wigwams, flattening crops and turning the whole area into a quagmire. Tribal leaders then chanted for the rain to stop. Chief Peter Rudd said, "We told the Great Spirit that we appreciated his generosity, but we had all we needed." Rain stopped two hours later.

Allah was even more prompt than the Great Spirit. When King Fahd called Muslims in Saudi Arabia together for a special ceremony to pray for rain, a heavy storm washed out the prayers before they could begin.

RAIN ALSO brought about the downfall of Italian priest Don Giacomo Perini. As he stood outside his church in Alto Adige cursing the rain, he was killed instantly when the foundations of a large cross in the churchyard were loosened by the deluge, causing it to crash down on his head.

COLLAPSING EDIFICES seem to be a common holy hazard. During September 1994, a five year old girl visiting her grandparents' grave in Paris was killed when her father leant on an old gravestone and it collapsed on top of her. During January of the same year Don Armani, a priest from Pavia, Italy, was slightly luckier. When he was erecting a 7-foot statue of the Virgin in his church, it collapsed on him, but he escaped with two broken legs. He apparently said, "God moves in mysterious ways but I can't imagine what this was supposed to tell me."

HUNDREDS OF PILGRIMS rushed to a Thai temple north-west of Bangkok after its Buddhist abbot announced that he had dreamt a god descended and made the soil a miracle cure. At least three people became seriously ill from eating the allegedly divine dirt.

THE HAJJ, the annual Muslim pilgrimage to Mecca, has an unenviable record for disaster. On 23 May 1994 between 200 and 1,000 Muslim pilgrims, depending on which report you read, were trampled to death. It happened during a ritual in which the pilgrims trek to Mina, 15 kilometres outside Mecca, to throw stones at three piles of rock which symbolise the Devil. According to reports thousands of pilgrims were packing a pedestrian overpass on the approach to the rocks when a new wave of people arrived, pushing forward. This set off a series of panics as the authorities tried to regain control, leading to mounting casualties as pilgrims were crushed underfoot.

It wasn't the first Hajj-related mass death. In 1991 248 Nigerian Muslims were killed when the plane they'd chartered crashed on take-off from Jeddah after they'd completed their Hajj, and earlier that year 92 Senegalese had died the same way. In the 1970s at least 700 pilgrims died in Hajj-related flying accidents and 301 pilgrims from Pakistan died in August 1980 in an incident between Jeddah and Riyadh. The worst tragedy took place in 1990 when 1500 people died of suffocation when a crowd panicked in an access tunnel. The only consolation for the bereaved – and possibly for the deceased – is that Muslims believe that if they die in Mecca, they will automatically go to heaven as martyrs.

A GULF STATE received a bill for 12,000 dirhams (£1,750) for drinks consumed by an official guest from his hotel room mini-bar in just four days in 1991. Investigating the charges, the civil servant responsible for paying the bill discovered that the guest in question was a Muslim leader who had been representing his nation at an Islamic conference. When asked if he had used the mini-bar in his room, he began cursing, "Those damned evil-doers! Every time I cleansed my room of the satanic munkar (alcohol) by smashing the bottles or pouring them down the loo, the devils refilled the icebox with more."

WILLIAM H. IRVING III thought God had answered his prayers when he received a cheque for $836,939.19 from the government. A few days before he had prayed to God for the means to support himself and his family and believed this was his answer. He spent more than $300,000 before the Treasury realised that they had made an error and had sent him considerably more than the $183.69 he was enti-tled to as a Gulf War veteran. He was promptly arrested and charged with fraud. The judge said he did not question Irving's religious faith, then gave him 46 months in prison.

CHAN WAI-FONG, aged 65, was outside her son's home in a Hong Kong apartment block, giving thanks to the gods for her daughter-in-law's lucky escape from a road accident, when she was struck and killed by a falling bag of cement.

ANOTHER SURPRISE FROM ABOVE was visited on 40 diplomats at the Pakistani Embassy in London as they sat cross legged on prayer mats in their mosque. Overhead, builders were taking up scaffolding planks placed across the glass roof so they could work on a neighbouring building when one of the team slipped and hurtled through the glass, falling 15 feet onto a shocked diplomat's foot. An Embassy spokesman said, "We shall be sending them the repair bill."

FOR OVER 90 YEARS a stained glass window had remained hidden behind the organ at All Saint's Church, Oystermouth, Mumbles until it was revealed by renovation work in 1994. The day before it was due to be officially unveiled a workman put a scaffolding pole straight through it, utterly wrecking it. The vicar, Canon Geoff Thomas, was appropriately forgiving. "It was just an accident. Stained glass is broken so easily," he said.

IF BELIEVING in God doesn't keep you out of trouble, neither, it seems, does actually being God. In February 1996 God was sent to prison for nine months by a judge in San Rafael, California, when he was found guilty of exposing himself to a woman in a coffee shop. God, aged 68, had been arrested 18 times in the past for similar offences and was considered to be suffering from a psychotic disorder by the court-appointed psychiatrist. "God is simply too sick to be out on the streets," she said.

Ubiquitous Perpetuity God, to give him his full name, was born as Enrique Silberg in Cuba, but emigrated to the US where he changed his name to his present, rather more cosmic moniker. He first came to prominence in 1986 after he was mugged by two men in San Francisco. They were arrested and found to be in possession of a passport and wallet belonging to "P. God". When police tried to trace him to swear out a complaint, God was found to have left his motel in a hurry, leaving no forwarding address.

Health Hazard

Hospitals are supposed to be places where you go to get better, but...

THE BRITISH MEDICAL JOURNAL published a report in 1988 which revealed that the greatest threat to medical staff's health is other medical staff. Surgeons often skewer themselves and their assistants with the orthopaedic pins used to fix fractures, with the most extreme example being a consultant who not only transfixed his assistant's hand, but also impaled the patient's other leg with the pin. Some doctors break their own bones by dropping traction weights on their feet and one stabbed a colleague in the stomach with his scalpel as he turned to explain a procedure to him.

The worst case seems to have been one where a mouse ran loose in an operating theatre, causing panic among nursing staff as it was pursued by the surgeon. It disappeared, but the patient, who was under local anaesthetic saw it and sat up shouting, "There it is!" This time the surgeon caught it, but on returning to the operation, failed to notice the lights had been lowered and knocked himself out on the rim of the operating table.

THE LIGHTS also brought grief to Avril Crossley as she lay on the operating table at North Tees Hospital, Cleveland. While she was under anaesthetic for orthopaedic surgery a heavy overhead light crashed down on her chest, causing severe bruising and preventing the surgeon from operating. A hospital spokesman said, "It appears to have been a manufacturing fault."

IN CAPETOWN a surgeon was sued by one of his patients after he apparently sewed the man's hands, amputated in an accident, back onto the wrong arms. At least they were his own hands, though. In Munich, a railway accident resulted in eleven men being seriously injured, with two losing their hands. Doctors retrieved the hands and managed to reattach them, unfortunately not to their original owners. The two men had identical blood types and the mistake was only discovered after surgery was complete. The hospital said "one of them wants his original hands back, but we're trying to talk him out of that."

A DUTCHMAN who went into hospital in 1992 to be circumcised awoke to be told he had been given a vasectomy because of a mix-up in patients' records. He got off comparatively lightly, though, compared with a soldier who went into a military hospital for a skin graft, but had his penis amputated instead. The soldier attempted suicide as a result and lived in "social seclusion" while suing the Ministry of Defence for damages.

IN DUBLIN a woman visited her doctor complaining of a bad cough and was prescribed antibiotics and cough mixture. He also gave her a "free sample" of the medicine. She returned four days later saying she felt extremely unwell and that she found the cough mixture "vile and sickening". On checking the bottle the doctor found he had mistakenly given her a urine sample left by another patient. She sued him for £22,000.

AFTER VISITING a London doctor complaining of dizziness and loss of balance, a woman was told she was suffering from syphilis. She was in fact suffering from wobbly shoes, and when she replaced them her problems vanished.

A 70-YEAR-OLD man died in flames while using oxygen in Ellesworth, Maine. He was a heavy smoker who used oxygen all the time to assist his breathing. He lit a cigarette with his oxygen compressor still running and inhaled, drawing oxygen through the cigarette and causing a flash fire which surged into his lungs, killing him instantly.

DOCTORS in Copenhagen spent two hours trying to prise two lovers apart after the braces on their teeth locked as they kissed passionately in a city cinema. A medic said, "It wouldn't have taken so long had they been able to stop laughing."

AFTER BEING BLIND for 20 years 64-year-old Gauri Banerjee accidentally hit his head against a door, a blow which miraculously restored his sight. The same blow, however, caused him to go completely deaf. Doctors in Ajmer, in India, were baffled as to how such dramatic changes could occur.

A door in the casualty department of Whipps Cross Hospital, East London, had a rather more predictable effect, it fell on a woman visiting for treatment to her swollen elbow and added facial bruising to her woes.

80-YEAR-OLD Dr. C. Dupha Reeves had been elected coroner of Wayne County, New York, for 26 consecutive years when he was asked to identify the bodies of Vickie Lee Evans and her son John, who had burned to death in a mobile home fire. He did not visit the scene of the fire, but duly identified the remains presented to him as those of Vickie and John. It was not until the child's father, Gary Rotondo, returned to the burnt-out caravan and found the boy's charred torso that anyone realised something had gone wrong. Reeves had misidentified the remains of a pet rabbit as those of one-year-old John. He admitted, "Because I was told a mother and child had died in the fire, I assumed it was the body of the child. I misidentified it."

A HAMBURG DOCTOR also had identification problems. He reported his white Volkswagen missing, but rang the police station three days later to say it had turned up. He told the police, "It was parked in the street all the time. I forgot it had been resprayed red."

TWO DETERMINED ambulance men went to the wrong address, grabbed a healthy Norwegian, slapped him onto a stretcher and rushed him to a hospital in Kragero, 40 miles away, despite his vociferous objections. Meanwhile the real patient, who had the same name and lived in the same village, despite suffering from severe anaemia, drove himself to the hospital, where he had problems registering because the clerk insisted he was already there.

JUST BEFORE going into surgery to have his foot amputated, Willie King joked with staff to be sure they knew which one they were going to take off. Surgeon Rolando Sanchez still got it wrong and King, a 51-year-old diabetic, awoke to find he still had his gangrenous right foot, but the healthy right one was missing. He eventually had both legs removed just below the knee and settled with the surgeon for $250,000. After the incident, the hospital started a new policy of writing "NO" on patients' limbs which are not to be amputated.

Rolando Sanchez, though, did not stop there. He later amputated a woman's toe while he was supposed to be removing dead tissue from her right foot. He later said that the toe "had fallen off". This time he was stripped of his licence.

DETECTIVES called to a disturbance outside a pub in Southampton found a severed ear, which they packed in ice and put in the police station fridge so that surgeons could reattach it when its owner was found. The next day its owner came forward, but had to be told that the ear had "gone off". Detective Inspector Ray Burt explained, "It was next to an egg roll and that had gone off as well, so there was nothing we could do."

Koto Salaki of Christchurch, New Zealand, was, from one point of view, luckier. After a drinking binge with friends, he passed out and the others decided to play a joke on him, so they stripped him naked and shaved off all his hair and eyebrows. When he didn't react, they decided to go further, so they cut off his ear and glued it to the middle of his forehead. When Koto came round and looked in the mirror he failed to see the funny side of coming face-to-face with a bald man with an ear on his forehead.

Surgeons were at least able to put the detached organ back in its correct place.

STAFF at the Centre for Devices and Radiological Health, part of the Food and Drug Administration in Washington, held a Christmas party on 14 December 1984. More than half the party-goers had nausea and other symptoms of food poisoning by the following Monday. They referred the matter to the appropriate authorities, their colleagues.

A MORBID FEAR of dentists drove Walter Hallas, a Leeds market stall assistant, to ask a workmate to cure his toothache with a punch on the jaw. The punch felled him, causing him to strike his head on the ground. He died later from a fractured skull.

It's a Lottery!

**Gambling is asking for bad luck,
but there's bad luck and then
there's really bad luck.**

DICE seem to be the most dangerous form of gambling, as just playing the game can be hazardous. Whenever Michel LaTruille went for a big throw during dice games in Paris, he normally blew on the dice for luck, but his luck ran out when he accidentally sucked instead, inhaled the dice and choked to death. Meanwhile in Puerto Rico another unfortunate gambler was blinded in his left eye when he threw his dice and one bounced up and struck him in the face.

AFTER A LIFETIME of fruitless raffle entries, balding Chris Calver of Jesmond, Newcastle finally struck lucky: he won some curling tongs. A similar joy awaited factory worker Eddie Horth from Bridlington, who entered a magazine contest while recovering from having his leg amputated – he won a pair of skates.

ROULETTE is one of the hardest games to beat the bank at, but Pauline Kale and her husband Kemal had a go. For almost 20 years they worked diligently on creating the perfect roulette system, never placing a bet without consulting notebooks they always carried at the tables, and taking into account the stars and phases of the Moon in their calculations.

They never did particularly well until one evening in 1977 when they played at the Palm Beach Casino in Cannes. All night the chips piled up and an admiring crowd gathered to watch them work the table, until by 3.30 a.m. they had amassed £30,000. They gave casino staff a £500 tip and went home. As they opened their front door three masked men leapt on them, grabbed the bag containing their night's winnings and fled. Mrs Kale said, "The win was a splendid triumph for us. In future we shall just play cards at home – for matches."

GETTING THE RIGHT lottery numbers once is hard enough, but to get the winning numbers in two different lotteries at the same time is almost impossible. Nonetheless, Maureen Wilcox did just that. She got the correct numbers for the Massachusetts and Rhode Island lotteries in the same week, but did not win a penny – her Massachusetts numbers won in Rhode Island and her Rhode Island numbers in Massachusetts.

CHENG PO-JEN, a school pupil from Southern Taiwan, won a brand-new Porsche in a radio competition. However, there were two other students named Cheng Po-Jen at the same school who also entered the contest, and no one knew which one the winner was, even after the student's entry forms were scrutinised by handwriting experts.

UNEMPLOYED CARPENTER Peter Reider, from Vienna, had only a few days to pay his debts or he would lose his car and furniture to the hire-purchase companies. Desperate, he donned a balaclava and robbed a bank in Graz with a toy pistol. As he toured Vienna, using the £4000 he had gained to pay off what he owed, his taxi driver thought he was acting suspiciously and informed police, who searched Reider's house and found the balaclava and pistol. He was charged with bank robbery, found guilty and jailed for five years. On his second day in prison his girlfriend visited him to tell him he had won £40,000 on the football pools.

IN LOS ANGELES, Kelly Ketchem won $58,000 on a TV game show which he had entered under an alias. This was not enough, though – he was recognised by viewers as a man wanted for a $100,000 fraud and arrested when he went to collect his winnings. A similar event caused the downfall of Vincente Brito de Queiroz in Brazil. He appeared on TV to collect his $5 million lottery winnings and was identified as a fugitive suspected of killing his wife.

CROSSWORD fanatic Dick Vowles did the *Observer*'s Everyman prize crossword every week for 66 years from its launch in 1927, with only a short break during his war service. Every week he sent his correct entry in, but never won a prize. Finally in 1993 luck shone upon him and he won a £15 book token. But Mr Vowles never knew: he had died, aged 84, the day before the newspaper sent him his prize.

FUNERAL HOME OWNER Edward Gardner won £650,000 on the New Jersey State Lottery, three weeks after he died. He had bought lottery tickets all his life, but his win was only announced after he died following a fall on a hunting trip. Clarence Kinder at least had a chance to enjoy winning his lottery prize, but not spending it. He won $50,000 by spinning the wheel on a televised lottery show in Charleston, West Virginia on 12 November 1987, but on Friday 13th he dropped dead of a heart attack. Sinisia Micic had even worse luck. He won £40,000 in a lottery in what was then Yugoslavia, and went out to celebrate in a local bar. At the end of the evening he lurched out into the street and was crushed by a passing lorry.

FRIDAY THE 13TH was also unlucky for Scott Wenner. On that day in January 1995 he bought a ticket for the Texas Lottery from a Pic-A-Tate outlet in the Philadelphia suburb of Croydon which won him $10 million, or should have. The Texas Lottery refused to cough up because Pic-A-Tate is not licensed to sell Texas Lottery tickets.

ALSO THWARTED in his attempt to claim his winnings was Arton Schmidt. Unemployed, he made a desperate attempt to win the German football pools by filling in 25,000 lines, for which he had to submit a £3900 stake. He should have won £98,000, but got nothing because his stake cheque had bounced. The same fate apparently also happened to another German, Enton Schwartz, after his £4750 cheque bounced, depriving him of a £297,000 win.

ANOTHER NEAR MISS was suffered by Susan Evans, who lost an £8.5 million jackpot on the British National Lottery when her boyfriend processed her ticket one second after the deadline. He got stuck behind another customer and the lottery machine closed down while printing her numbers. Guiseppe Bonacle of Ascoli Piceno, Italy also missed out on his win when he entrusted his lottery ticket purchase to someone else. Bonacle had used the same numbers for an amazing 71 years, but when they finally came up, he got nothing. That week he was ill and had asked his daughter to buy his ticket. She forgot. Paul Manarang had no one to blame but himself. He won £85,000 on the California Lottery. Having 180 days to claim his prize, he turned up for it on the 181st.

WINNING A CAR was all too much for Janet Keedwell of Pontygwaith, Wales. She was so shocked by the news that she was struck down by neuralgia and was too ill to pick up her prize. Conrado Bacani's prize car brought problems of a different kind. He won the second-hand vehicle in a raffle in the Philippines, but when he tried to register it he was arrested for possessing a stolen car. It had been reported as stolen some years before, but had never been recovered. Police were forced to release Bacani after they found it had been donated to the raffle by a local police chief. An investigation was launched into why the car had been in police possession for years.

HELL BECKONED for Maria Benoiza Nascimento, an unemployed cleaner and mother of seven, if she continued to play the lottery, according to her preacher, so she burned the ticket she had. That week her numbers came up, and if she'd still had the ticket she would have won £40,000. She may have saved her soul, but her husband beat her and left home when he found out what had happened.

Upendranath Roy, a poverty-stricken sawmill worker from Delhi, missed out on a life of luxury when his wife tore up his winning tickets. He had copied the numbers onto a piece of paper and hidden the tickets under his bed, but when he rushed home to get them after the results were announced he found that his wife had discovered them when clearing up and, thinking they were useless, had binned them. He searched the dustbins and found a fragment with the first four digits, but not the rest.

ALSO SEARCHING through garbage was Dale Miller of Florida, who bought a winning lottery ticket worth $6.6 million. On discovering his win Miller held a night of heavy celebration which culminated in a furious row with his wife. He stormed out of the house, returning at noon the next day to find his wife had tidied the house to make amends, throwing out all the rubbish from the festivities – including the winning ticket. Miller spent more than two weeks fruitlessly combing the local rubbish tip for his missing fortune, and when asked what he would spend the money on if he ever found it said, "clean clothes and a divorce."

DIVORCE was not needed by Terry Milner, as his lottery ticket purchase meant he was left standing at the altar. He bought his fiancée Helen Borton a block of lottery tickets a few days before their wedding, and when she didn't turn up for the ceremony Terry raced round to her flat, to find a note saying one of the tickets had won her £3 million. This made her realise she didn't want to be his wife after all, so she'd gone off on a round-the-world trip on her own.

BUS DRIVER James Troy hit lottery trouble in Augusta, Philadelphia. Already 15 minutes behind schedule, Troy parked his bus outside a store and joined the queue for lottery tickets. Inside the store was the transit company's operations manager Nora Roberts, who told him to get back on his bus and continue his route. Troy told her he would when he'd got his tickets. She fired him.

CHAPTER TEN

Destiny Calling

Many people believe names have a power all of their own – for some their name is their doom.

JASON LUCK, a Worthing lifeguard, aged 22, was finally killed after suffering a catalogue of accidents. He fell out of a moving train and over a viaduct, surviving that, he also managed to fall out of a high window at the hospital he was taken to. This left him paralysed and on a life-support machine, the alarm of which failed to sound when a tube came loose, finally causing his demise. Bad luck, clearly.

SARAH CARELESS, 26, from Tamworth in Staffordshire, was given a Peugeot 306 Cabriolet as an anniversary present. On her first journey in it she was involved in a head-on crash. She escaped injury, but the repair bill was over £2,000. Another Careless, this time James Careless of Wolverhampton, was crushed and killed when his vehicle overturned while he was driving along a beach in Lanzarote.

FLEETUS LEE GOBBLE, aged 45, choked to death on food in the K&W Cafeteria in Winston-Salem, North Carolina. In Nairobi a man walked into a supermarket, gulped down two bottles of whisky and put a third in his pocket. Amazingly he was still able to lurch out of the shop, but was swiftly arrested. His name was Charles Wanjohi Hinhu, which in his native Kikuyu language means "Charles of the Quick Drink".

KATHLEEN CROOK, a magistrate in Bournemouth, was charged with submitting false claims for loss of earnings and expenses while sitting on the bench in February 1994 – though she insisted she was innocent. Another public official, Congressman Pat Swindall of Georgia, lived up to his name when he was arrested on corruption charges, which brings us to shipping office manager Thomas Gilbert Swindells who was done for fraud in 1980.

CHRIS AND JACKIE FLOOD drenched their home in Buckinghamshire three times in three months. Their 45-gallon fishtank burst twice and Chris put a nail through a water pipe. Jackie said, "I think our name is jinxed."

THEATRE-GOERS attending performances at the newly opened Glasgow Citizen's Theatre in 1992 had to negotiate buckets catching drips from leaking roofs caused by high winds and torrential rain. The shows they were going to see were Craig Raine's *1953* and Alonso Alegria's *Niagara*. At the Playhouse in Edinburgh, a production of *Singing in the Rain* was abandoned after a fault in the sprinkler system poured hundreds of gallons of water into the building.

TWO DUTCHMEN put to sea in a yacht called 'Chaos' in 1991. They had no charts and got lost off Dorset. They called up the coastguard to find out where they were – and their radio broke down. They were eventually found by a lifeboat and towed into Poole harbour. In 1981 a 32-foot fishing vessel was rammed by a whale about 20km off the coast of Massachusetts. As the boat began to sink, the three-man crew was rescued by the coastguard. The boat's name was 'Shattered'. Photographer Struan Wallace, meanwhile, bought a houseboat called 'Atlantis', moored on the Thames at Brentford. It sank.

A PLUMBER had to be freed by firemen after he got his head stuck in a lavatory bowl at his home in Puckeridge, Hertfordshire – his name was W.C. Sticks.

FOUR MEMBERS of the Cardiff rock group Violent Storm were killed and a fifth seriously injured when their car smashed into a bridge during a violent storm on the M4 Motorway near Bristol on Friday 13th March 1992. It is believed that a freak gust of wind lifted their car six feet into the air and hurled it against a bridge support, causing it to land upside down.

DURING STORMS in January 1990 an 80-foot pine tree crashed down onto Maurice Harvey's house in Torquay, causing £60,000 worth of damage. The house was named Pine Falls.

LILLIAN SLOMAN, aged 91, was congratulated for having a clean driving record for 70 years, then banned for driving too slowly by a magistrate in Worthing, after delaying two policemen by driving at 15mph in a 60mph speed limit. At Newbury in Berkshire, cyclist Terry Clout was knocked off his bike by motorist Alexander Dent, but not seriously hurt.

A DUTCH LORRY overturned, spilling a ton and a half of eels on the road near Stonycross in the New Forest after hitting a car with the number plate EEL293V.

SANDRA BLEWITT failed to become the first woman to swim the north channel between Northern Ireland and Scotland when she was defeated by the cold, rough seas and jellyfish stings. This was not the first time she had blown it either: in 1980 she failed to swim the English Channel four times.

NOTHING was left of Nothing on 5 July 1988, after fire swept through the tiny desert community, a service stop on Route 93 in Arizona, which had a resident population of four.

NICHOLAS FORLETTA, aged 24, of Torquay was fined £200 for swearing at police during an altercation in April 1986. Cardiff Crown Court had occasion to imprison Neil and Teresa Tantrum of Rhondda, Mid-Glamorgan, for affray in 1994. Mr and Mrs Tantrum had gone to Tonyrefail Comprehensive after their daughter had complained that she was being bullied. Mrs Tantrum yanked hair from one girl's head and chipped her tooth while Mr Tantrum yelled obscenities.

Oops!

Accidents are never much fun, but more than a few come with a hideous twist.

TRAVEL AGENT Charles Larrain was killed after ducking to avoid a paper aeroplane thrown by a colleague in his Paris office. He banged his head on a desk, collapsed, and died in the ambulance on the way to hospital.

SKY-DIVER Ivan McGuire, 35, filmed his two-mile death fall after jumping from an aircraft near Louisberg, North Carolina without his parachute on. He did, however, have a camera attached to his helmet, which survived. Film from it shows other sky-divers free-falling, but disappearing abruptly as their parachutes open, leaving McGuire to continue his plunge. "A man who has jumped 800 times ought to remember his parachute," police said.

ANOTHER EMBARRASSING aerial accident was suffered by Captain Craig Fisher of the US Air Force while flying an

F-16 fighter. Needing to take a pee, he got out the "Piddle Pack" – a sponge filled plastic pouch – from the pocket of his flight suit, unhooked his lap belt, unzipped his suit and raised himself up on the seat ready to fire... then lost control of the aircraft. The F-16 was travelling at 345 mph at 28,000 feet when Fisher bailed out, leaving £11.2 million of jet to crash near Palmdale Air Terminal in California.

FEARING another attack by the Unabomber, California State University called in the Los Angeles County Bomb Squad to deal with a package, which had aroused suspicion because it was bulky and had no return address. The bomb squad moved it to a nearby field and as TV news helicopters circled they detonated the package, sending a flurry of white papers into the air. They had just blown up Takash Kawai's music thesis, containing a bulky manuscript and a cassette which he had sent in for submission. Fortunately Kawai had a duplicate, and was given extra time to resubmit his work.

Not so lucky was Professor Keith Robbins from the University of Wales. He had put together a 1000-page bibliography of modern British history, taking 15 years over the task and sent the only copy off to the publishers – where it was binned by the cleaners. Professor Robbins, described as "gutted" by the event, was able to salvage the situation by piecing it back together from photocopies and bits saved on computer disk, but it was a close call.

PHOTOGRAPHY turns out to be more hazardous than one might expect, according to the next three tales. Visiting the castle of San Giovanni in Italy, 18-year-old Roberto Lorenzato tried to take a picture of his fiancée, Stefani Ferrazza, 17, standing on the castle wall. To fit her in the viewfinder he asked her to take a step back. She did – and plummeted 50ft to her death. Antonio Baroni was luckier. He was standing on the rim of a volcano on the Italian island of Eoile when he was asked to take a step back for a photo, and plunged 100ft into the volcano. He escaped unhurt.

The photographer doesn't always get away with it, though. An amateur photographer who asked, not surprisingly, to remain anonymous, was setting up a shot on the cliff at Cemaes Head near Cardigan in Wales when he stepped back to improve the shot and dropped 60ft down the cliff-face, breaking his leg. Coastguards had to rescue him from a ledge.

TWO LAWYERS in New York decided to settle a friendly argument about the record time for the Olympic 100 metres by racing down one of the corridors of their office. One of them, however, had forgotten his contact lenses and overshot the end of the corridor, shooting out through a 39th-floor window to his death.

MOTORIST Abner Kriller of Albany, Australia, came to a sticky end while trying to drive and chew gum at the same time. He blew a huge chewing gum bubble which burst in his face, coating it with goo and temporarily blinding him. He missed a bend and went straight over a cliff.

WHISTLING MILKMAN Geoff Fry lost his chance at winning a national award after a DIY disaster. He was using an electric sander when he slipped and fell face-first onto the still running machine. His lips swelled up and he could no longer pucker them to whistle, forcing him to pull out of the contest to find Britain's Most Melodious Milkman.

A grimmer fate awaited World Yo-Yo champion Ted Gerner. He was practising his skills in a public park in

Sydney, Australia, when one of his tricks went horribly wrong. He was twirling a wooden yo-yo around his head at speeds close to 80mph, when he lost control, allowing the speeding device to smash into his head, killing him on the spot.

A £5000 BANNER welcoming visitors to a Washington public library in 29 languages had to be taken down in a hurry after a Filipino security guard at the library spotted that the word that was supposed to say "Greetings" to his fellow countrymen actually said "Circumcision".

AN EGYPTIAN BUTCHER was jailed for a year for killing a three-year-old girl while trying to restore her lost voice with a cleaver. People in some parts of the country believe a lost voice can be restored if a butcher passes the blunt edge of his cleaver along the patient's throat. The butcher from El-Kharkaniya got the right general idea, but got a little lost in the detail – he used the sharp edge.

A FIRE-EATER who had a coughing fit during his act in Munich got more than he bargained for. The 35-year-old Rastafarian accidentally spat petrol onto his beard and dread-locks, and seconds later they burst into flame, leaving his head a raging inferno. He was rushed to hospital with severe burns.

THE PETERBOROUGH *Evening Telegraph* was forced to abandon its first spot-the-ball competition in February 1995 after the picture was published with the ball still in it. This palls in the face of a publication error made by *Larousse*, France's most renowned dictionary. Under 'champignons', three poisonous mushrooms were listed as harmless, includ-

ing the deathcap, which is fatal. 180,000 dictionaries were
withdrawn at a cost of £3 million and copies with the error
immediately became collectors' items.

THE BOTTLE of 1787 Chateau Margaux bought by New
York wine merchant Bill Sokolin was a collectors' item,
until Bill got his hands on it. As he celebrated purchasing
the wine, which had once belonged to US President Thomas
Jefferson, in a restaurant, a waiter brushed past and the
antique claret crashed to the floor, leaving a £400,000 stain
on the carpet. When Sokolin tasted a salvaged mouthful, he
had to admit that it was "not very good".

SIX PEOPLE were hospitalised in Sussex after an accident
in a Brighton swimming pool changing room. After shower-
ing, one of the swimmers mistook a CS-gas self-defence
spray for his deodorant and filled the men's changing room
with fumes.

CARLTON TV had to refund British Airways £6,000 after
it ran one of the airline's adverts in the middle of an air disaster movie. BA officials were furious when the TV station
ran their ad immediately after scenes of mid-air horror in
the film *Terror In the Sky*. The Australian airline Quantas, on
the other hand, had to abandon its £1 million advertising
campaign after an Australian recognised the sun-drenched
beach where it was filmed. It was in Hawaii. Film of the
wrong beach had been used in order to save money, and it
was thought that no one would notice. "It was an error of
judgement," said a spokesman.

BALD Alan Turner invested £6,500 in a hair transplant
which involved having 6,000 synthetic hairs grafted onto his

pate. His joy in having a shiny new hairstyle literally vanished when he tried to wash it in the shower. As he shampooed the threads they came out in handfuls and were washed down the plughole, leaving him with scarcely a hundred strands in place. "I am devastated, now I won't go out without a hat on," said the downcast Turner. The clinic responsible admitted the operation had been a failure and gave him a complete refund.

IN 1975 Honduran peasant Gustavo Adolfo Amador was charged with stealing coloured pencils from a marketplace in the capital of Tegucigalpa, but a court acquitted him the following year. The written release order, however, did not arrive at Tegucigalpa's central penitentiary where Gustavo was being held, and he remained there until April 1994 when the error was discovered, 19 years late.

AS A PRESENT for his wife, Jochen Menkel, 56, bought a £2,400 diamond-studded brooch and tied it to the string of a helium-filled party balloon. On the way home, however, he stumbled over the doorstep of his house in Germany and let go of the balloon, which promptly ascended to the heavens. A police spokesman said, "We have alerted other police forces in the balloon's flightpath, but we don't have much hope of recovering the brooch."

IN A SIMILARLY UNWISE move with her valuables, Lilian Sokolowsky hid £14,000 worth of jewellery in a fake soup can in order to fool thieves. She then gave the can away to the Salvation Army who were collecting food for the homeless.

The Road To Hell

...is paved with good intentions

TWO MEN waiting for an airdrop of Red Cross supplies to starving refugees in Sudan were killed by falling food bags.

CONVICTED THIEF Wilma Jean Kanflee found apologising to one of her victims much harder than she ever imagined. When she called at Mr Turner Gwyn's house in Wilkesboro, North Carolina, he refused to open the door. Ms Kanflee, undeterred and determined to apologise face-to-face, broke it down. Mr Gwyn shot her three times, seriously injuring her.

TO SAVE MONEY Moray House College, a teacher-training college in Edinburgh, launched an energy conservation study. The result unearthed an electricity meter hidden behind a locked basement door, which had not been read for fourteen years, landing the college with a potential bill of many thousands of pounds.

FIREMEN ANSWERING an emergency call at the home of Richard Derrick in Taunton arrived just as Mr Derrick's 80-gallon tropical fish tank exploded. This put out the fire, but left 60 tropical fish floundering on the carpet. The firemen scooped them up and threw them into another tank which had remained intact. This turned out to be home to Percy the Piranha, who promptly ate 57 of them.

AUTHORITIES IN San Rafael, California, built the world's first subsidised apartment block for people sensitive to soap, cosmetics and household cleaners. The first residents moved into the chemical-free Ecology House and immediately became violently ill. They were all moved out again as officials tried to track down the source of the foul smell causing the problem. The British Migraine Association dropped a similar clanger when it sent 13,000 car stickers out to members. The smell of the ink on them was enough to spark instant migraine attacks in many sufferers, with at least one collapsing just from opening the envelope.

TO COOL his house on the Greek island of Corfu, Christos Bertsos went for a radical solution. He installed the 12-foot propeller from an aircraft engine as a cooling fan. When he switched it on, it blew the roof of his house off.

THREE HUNDRED TONS of sand were put down to make a new bathing beach at Burnham-on-Crouch, Essex. It disappeared when the tide went out.

SEEING HER NEIGHBOUR being mugged by two men in

Kensington High Street while looking out of her upstairs window, a woman threw a heavy glass at them. It hit the victim on the head, knocking her senseless. The muggers grabbed her handbag and fled.

A BOWLING CLUB met with dismal failure when it tried to rid its greens of marauding rabbits by bringing in the exterminators. They only caught and strangled one rabbit, the club's black mascot, called Lucky. The animal had been adopted by players at the club in Torquay when they were on a losing streak, and it had been credited with bringing about an upturn in their fortunes. After it died, the bad luck returned. Embarrassingly, one of the exterminators who offed the unfortunate bunny was a member of the club.

EXTERMINATORS also brought grief to the Kay family of Philadelphia when they came round to destroy a termite infestation. They drilled a hole in the basement floor and ruptured a fuel line, causing a major oil leak which produced a variety of damage which cost $400,000 to put right. Michael Kay said, "I had fully tiled rooms in the basement, a bar, laundry room and pantry, now all I've got is oil and dirt. They've dug 55 inches below the original floor and they're not done yet." Fumes got so bad that Kay and his family had to flee to a nearby motel while the repair work was done. "It's just one thing after another," he said. "Today they told me the oil's outside the house."

A DRASTIC SOLUTION to a mosquito problem was adopted by Jaques Boufell. He decided to burn them out of his house in France with a flamethrower. The flames caused a gas explosion which destroyed the house and put Boufell in hospital... but it did kill all the mosquitoes.

A SUSPICIOUS BOX found outside Bristol Zoo prompted a call to the bomb disposal squad. After it was blown up, it was found to have contained a rat left by its owner who was looking for a new home for his pet. In Newcastle upon Tyne, someone dropped off a box of kittens at an animal refuge for rehoming, but left in such a hurry that they drove over the box, killing two of the three cats inside.

THE POLICE have a particularly appalling record when it comes to animal welfare, if our files are anything to go by. In Sunderland, PC Steve Hansom was called to deal with a dispute between two neighbours over a pet cat called Pepsi, during which Paul Tansey was accused of hitting Scott Marshall with a screwdriver. PC Hansom calmed the situation and arrested Tansey, but failed to notice that the cat had taken refuge under his panda car during the commotion. As he reversed the car to return to the police station, he drove straight over Pepsi, killing her instantly. Tansey burst into tears and had to be comforted by the policeman.

No better luck was had by PC Francis from Cheshire. He stopped his panda car to shoo away a cat that was stalking a baby sparrow, only to drive over the bird as he left, and in Lothian, in Scotland, a policeman sent to keep the peace between huntsmen and saboteurs managed to unite the two sides against him when he ran over the fox in his patrol car. Lest it be thought the animals get all the stick, spare a thought for policewoman Judith Mann, of Leiston. While rescuing a cat which had been run over, she lifted the animal into her car to take it to a vet. It sank its teeth into her, giving her severe blood poisoning.

A WHALE carcass that washed up on the beach of Florence, Oregon sometime in the 1970s caused problems for the Oregon State Highway Division, whose task it was to remove the rotting beast. After much deliberation it was decided to blow the whole thing up with a half-ton of dynamite, blasting it to fragments small enough for seagulls to eat. On the day chosen for the momentous event a large crowd gathered at the beach, along with a film crew who recorded the event for the local news and posterity. The film showed the whale being engulfed in a huge gout of smoke and flame, and the crowd cheering wildly for a few seconds before the cheers turned to screams and a new "splud" sound could be heard. What went up came straight down, and the bits of shredded whale rained down over a quarter of a mile, sending the panicking crowd fleeing for safety. A chunk of blubber caved in the roof of a parked car some distance from the beach. What's more, the whale corpse remained semi-intact as a sagging bridge over a prodigious crater, and not a seagull could be seen anywhere.

Long regarded as a particularly fanciful urban legend, the truth of this event was proved when the actual news film was posted to an Internet web site in 1995.

A WOMAN came home to find her husband frantically shaking in the kitchen with what looked like a wire running from his waist towards the electric kettle. assuming he was being electrocuted, she picked up a heavy piece of wood and smashed it into him to jolt him away from the current, breaking his arm in two places. Then she discovered he was listening to his walkman and having a jig.

ROMEO Sal Aspione hit upon a novel way to propose to his fiancée, Sara Rizzi. He slipped the engagement ring into her glass of champagne − only to watch in horror as she choked to death on it. Sal, a salesman in Sassari, Italy, said,

"I wanted to do something special for the woman I loved." Slightly better luck, but only slightly, was had by Curt Crew of Omaha, Nebraska, who asked a waitress to serve up a $2000 surprise engagement ring in his girlfriend's dessert. She gave it to the wrong woman and Crew could only watch helplessly as the stranger pocketed the ring and swiftly left with her own boyfriend.

FIFTY VILLAGERS in Southern Taiwan who took part in a firewalking ceremony across burning charcoal in order to bring wealth and good luck were hospitalised with burns.

A GOOD SAMARITAN who gave mouth-to-mouth resuscitation to a woman knocked down by a vehicle in Park Lane, Mayfair, had to be urgently tracked down by police because the woman, a drug addict, was suffering from infectious hepatitis.

A PATERNITY SUIT backfired on a hitch-hiker in Israel who got pregnant after having sex with a driver who picked her up. She spent three years tracing him in order to claim child support. This was the first time he had heard that their brief encounter had made him a father, and since he and his wife were childless after 20 years of marriage, he successfully counter-sued for custody of the child.

Serves 'Em Right

What may seem like tough shit may, in fact, simply be the serving of just desserts

ALIENS LANDED in Warrington, Cheshire, in 1993, or so several amateur radio enthusiasts believed. They were illegally eavesdropping on police frequencies with scanning equipment when they picked up messages about a huge glowing spacecraft which had crash-landed in a field, along with the warning "Do not approach, it might be radioactive" and directions to the field. Within minutes five radio hams had arrived at the site, where they were greeted by police, who arrested them for telecommunications offences.

TWO ANIMAL RIGHTS protesters were trampled to death by 2,000 pigs outside a slaughterhouse in Bonn. The pigs stampeded after a fence broke at a giant meat-packing plant.

IN SACRAMENTO, CALIFORNIA, David Vasquez spent $8 on an M-100 firecracker, an illegal firework three inches long and one inch wide, with an explosive power equal to one-eighth of a stick of dynamite. He lit it and attempted to throw it out of the window of his Cadillac, but missed. It hit the window frame and bounced back into the car, falling onto the floor between Vasquez's legs, where it exploded, blowing a chunk off his testicles. Recovering at the UC-Davis Medical Centre, he said, "It messed me up pretty bad." Police decided not to press charges.

A THIEF in Kisumu, Kenya, reversed the old adage "out of the frying pan, into the fire" when fleeing from an angry mob. In a bid for freedom he leapt from a window — straight into a street vendor's frying pan of sizzling oil.

A SNEAK thief in Zimbabwe attempted to steal food from the animals in Harare Zoo, but came badly unstuck when he tried to take meat from the lion enclosure. Zoo owner Vivian Bristow said, "All they left was some bones, an identity card and a driving licence."

WILFRED GENUS tried to avoid his 15-day jail sentence by persuading his friend Albert Flowers to serve it for him. Flowers agreed and began serving Genus's sentence in his place. All would probably have gone fine, if Genus had not decided to visit Flowers in jail, where he was caught carrying cocaine and a loaded handgun. This resulted in him facing a further ten years in jail for these offences while Flowers was charged with "impersonating another in order to serve a sentence" for which he could get a year in jail himself. Announcing Genus's arrest, Sheriff's Deputy Gabe Ramirez said, "These are not rocket scientists." Clive Lewis, meanwhile, was released from jail in Chicago after a five year stretch for robbery, and had his suitcase stolen on the way home.

TREES SEEM to be the chosen instruments of justice in Italy, where all these tales come from. After five years of having his drive blocked by a 70-year-old magnolia tree, which his neighbour Rino Poma refused to move, Giovanni Bignami finally reached the end of his tether. After a storming row with Poma, Bignami took an axe to the tree and felled it. Poma had the last laugh though, as the venerable tree toppled straight onto Bignami's new car and crushed it.

Giuseppi Lionello of Torreglia also got his come-uppance from a tree. Driven to fury by pigeons fouling his car from an overhanging bough, he chopped the tree down to stop it happening once and for all. This time the crashing tree spared the car – it fell on Giuseppi instead, killing him instantly.

Armando Pinelli had a row with another man in a park in Foggia over who should get the only chair in the shade of a palm tree. He only had a few moments to savour his victory: the palm keeled over and crushed him almost as soon as he had sat down.

Finally, in Milan, Ruggero Soldati shinned up a tree to avoid revenue officials who had come to see him about tax evasion. The effort, however, gave him violent cramp, which made him fall out of the tree, killing him. His reported last words were: "The cramp got me, not the tax men."

SHOULD ANYONE think vengeance by trees is a purely Italian phenomenon, here is an incident from elsewhere. In 1868 a Bristol mason, William Thorne, stole a fellow workman's tools. He did not get to keep them long: they were returned to their owner after a few hours when Thorne was killed by a falling tree and the tools were found on him.

IN SWANSEA a disgruntled customer hurled a rubber plant at the window of a food takeaway – it bounced off.

HANG-GLIDING is a fairly hazardous sport, but it became considerably more so near Trieste due to the presence of a large nudist colony frequented by attractive young women. Three hang-gliders took to circling the site to ogle the women, but this distracted them so much from their flying that all three collided in mid-air and crashed to the sand in front of the nudists. Two of the pilots were badly injured, the third was released after a check-up.

IRAQI TERRORIST Khay Rahnajet badly misjudged things when he attempted a letter bombing. He did not pay enough postage on his package for it to reach his intended victim. Instead it came back with "Return to Sender" stamped on it and exploded when Rahnajet picked it up. A Madrid postman had no better luck. He stole a parcel from work, took it home and opened it. Unfortunately this too was a letter bomb which blew up, seriously injuring his wife. Police charged him with theft.

A 14-YEAR-OLD VANDAL made a grave mistake when he tried to desecrate a cemetery in Chesham, Bucks. While wrecking tombs he managed to pull a gravestone over on top of himself, breaking his leg and pinning him to the ground, where he lay until a passer-by alerted police.

A GAY-BASHER got his just desserts when during a routine HIV test for an insurance application, it was found that he had AIDS. The 49-year-old truck driver from Nebraska had regularly beaten up gay men with a gang of friends during the six years he had worked in New York and New Jersey. Since he had been married to his wife for 25 years, had never been unfaithful and had never injected drugs, doctors concluded he had contracted the disease from one of his victims. The man admitted he often got large amounts of blood over him during the assaults, and at the time of his examination had scabs on his knuckles from a recent fight.

In Chicago two alleged rapists punched the air in victory when told they were to be freed because their victim had failed to turn up at court to testify against them. They became more subdued when they were told her absence was due to the fact that she was suffering from AIDS.

IN PERTH, Australia, a man had to have hospital treatment after "welding" his nylon underpants to his groin when he urinated on the power cable of an electric train. The 21-year-old man received the 25,000-volt shock while "train-surfing" with a friend.

IN ROMANIA, Fibis Carei tried to avoid the bother of a lengthy traditional slaughter when the time came to kill his pig Googo for Christmas dinner. Instead he wired up a mat of chicken wire to the local power grid and made Googo walk onto it. When the jolt of electricity hit it, the pig shot 10 feet into the air and crashed down on Fibis, seriously injuring him. Googo survived. Fibis was luckier than an elderly Texan who wanted to make his seven-stone goat "mean". He beat it regularly with a heavy stick. The goat gored him to death.

A 38-STONE Argentinean died after eating an 80-pound

piglet to win a bet. "Pablo de Casas was always boasting about how much he could eat, this time his stomach stretched so much he bled to death," said an unsympathetic coroner. Another competitive consumption bout did for an 18-year-old in Singapore. He entered a public smoking competition to see who could smoke the most cigarettes in three hours. He won, but dropped dead backstage while his name was being announced to the audience.

A Bullet With Your Name On

People are capable of generating the most appalling screw-ups without any help, but give them a weapon and they can really make a mess of things.

A RABBI accidentally shot a colleague with a harpoon-like cattle-slaughtering device at a meatpacking plant in Sandusky, Ohio. Avrohom Greenberg and Samuel Eldelman were overseeing the slaughter of animals at the plant, to ensure it was properly kosher, when Greenberg accidentally fired the weapon into Eldelman's abdomen.

MILTON ASHFORD AND LUVENIA WISE were found dead in bed, killed by a single bullet fired from a .44-calibre pistol in Columbia, South Carolina. The Richland County Coroner said, "It is my opinion that the pistol discharged accidentally during sexual intercourse. I'm convinced he did not intend to kill her." In Logan, Ohio, a man named only as Harry, awoke to the sound of what he thought were intruders in his room and opened fire on them from a supine position, sending a .32-calibre bullet through his penis and into the calf of his left leg.

PEOPLE WHO DO THIS sort of thing seem very reluctant to give their full names. A North Vancouver man called Fred belonged to a shooting club which allowed him to legally own the .357 Magnum revolver which was jammed down the front of his trousers as he swayed home from the pub one evening in 1983. About 20 minutes later, as he walked into the family home, his mother heard a shot and Fred came into the kitchen and sat down. At first there was no inkling that anything had gone wrong, but a few minutes later Fred admitted that he had shot himself. The Magnum had accidentally fired while tucked in Fred's waistband, blowing his left testicle off. Doctors saved the testicle and Fred recovered in hospital.

THE MAYOR OF CANDABA in the northern Philippines was less lucky. He should have known better than to wander about with a cocked pistol in his belt, but he did, and when he climbed into his official car one morning he accidentally slammed the door on it causing it to go off. His driver tried to rush him to the hospital but the car ran out of petrol on the way and he bled to death.

Also a victim of unwise holstering was hitman Chanh Thong Vo, who was himself victim of a contract killing in Toronto in December 1995. During his life he favoured his front waistband for holstering his handgun, and due to an earlier accident was known as No Wang Vo.

AN OLD MAN from Shreveport, suffering from kidney disease and in dialysis, finally lost his rag with bickering relatives and pulled a gun on them. While he was waving it threateningly in their direction, it accidentally went off, severing the tube from his dialysis machine. He bled to death.

IN PARIS, wealthy restaurant owner Douadi Mihoubi, 51, was bending over his car in a petrol station when he dropped his James Bond-style pen gun, just six inches long, which he carried to protect himself against muggers. The gun went off, shooting him through the heart and killing him instantly.

A BULLET fired accidentally by a man unloading his rifle went through his wall, across a yard and into another flat, in Oregon, USA, where it killed Marni Brooks, 23, who was lying in bed.

Fritz Gruber pulled a similarly inadvertent trick in Andernach, Germany. As he cleaned his rifle, it suddenly went off, blasting through the ceiling and shooting a burglar in the flat above.

AFTER HIS CAT crapped on the floor, a New York man tried to swat it with the butt of his shotgun, but the weapon was loaded and went off, shooting him dead. Farmer Alex Colleghagi from Bellusco, Italy was after a fox in a chicken shed with his shotgun, but when he fired it hit a support beam which fell and killed him.

AN ASTHMA ATTACK had unforeseen consequences for Vicki Childress, 38, of Key West, Florida. She slept with both her asthma inhaler and a .38-caliber revolver under her pillow. One night, suffering from an asthma attack, she reached under her pillow for relief. Her hand closed on the wrong item and she fired a bullet into her jaw, destroying some of her teeth.

DESPERATE for a cure for his raging toothache, farm labourer Francisco Asis dos Santos was actually trying to shoot out some teeth when he put his pistol to his mouth and pulled the trigger, aiming at the aching tooth. Even at point-blank range he still managed to miss, shooting out one of his eyes instead.

IN PLAINSVILLE, Ohio, Robert Heinbaugh gained the dubious distinction of being the first man ever to be shot by a lawnmower. As he cut his lawn he ran over a live bullet hidden in the grass which went off and shot him in the foot.

CHRISTMAS NIGHT 1995 had surprises in store for Richard Gardner, 23, and his wife beyond those brought by Santa. As he was nailing up some moulding at his mother-in-law's house in Lancaster, South Carolina, he shot himself in the hand and his wife in the stomach. He had thought the .25-calibre handgun he was using as a makeshift hammer was empty. It wasn't.

WHEN A FORTUNE-TELLER in Naples forecast that one of his clients would go to jail, the man was so enraged by the prediction that he pulled out a gun and shot the sooth-sayer — for which he was jailed. In Tanzania, witch-doctor Manu Urassa claimed to have concocted a potion which made him bulletproof, but was shot dead while testing it.

IN YVERDON, Switzerland, a 28-year-old man attempted to commit suicide with an assault rifle. He failed, and in frustration emptied the rest of the magazine out of the window, killing a janitor. "You must be one of the first potential suicides to miss with an assault rifle and 24 bullets," commented the judge at his trial. Tokyo student Oshi

Okawa should have been so lucky: he killed himself playing Russian roulette, but the odds were stacked against him — he used an automatic pistol.

PROFESSOR MARVO, a magician in Argentina, came to a sticky end when one of his tricks was just too believable for his own good. Performing to a small crowd in a tavern in Azul, he climaxed his act by catching a bullet, fired by his assistant, in his teeth. In reality the assistant fired a blank and the magician merely produced a bullet he had hidden in his mouth, but this subtlety was missed by Marco Asprella, a 48-year-old gold miner in the audience, who was so impressed by the trick that he whipped out his own .45-calibre handgun and yelling, "Catch this one Professor," fired it straight into Marvo's face, almost blowing his head off. He was stunned that he had killed the magician and all through his trial made it clear that he didn't understand why the man hadn't caught his bullet. The jury sympathised and acquitted him of the charge of murder. He was still found guilty of carrying a concealed weapon, for which he received a small fine and probation.

MORE PEOPLE do spectacularly stupid things while hunting than anyone could believe possible. On the isle of Elba in 1982, a young German tourist in a fur sleeping bag was shot dead by a hunter who mistook him for a wild boar. Near Chichester a hunter saw something white move in the grass, mistook nude sunbather Alan Fox for a rabbit, and shot him.

A SIMILAR PROBLEM led the Nova Scotia Forestry Commission to advise hunters to make sure their toilet paper is coloured. The odd recommendation followed an incident in which a hunter concealed himself in a bush to answer the call of nature. Another hunter mistook the flash of white lavatory paper for the tail of a deer and shot him dead.

EVEN THE EXPERTS get it wrong sometimes. Rob Manes, a safety expert for the Kansas Game Commission was wearing an orange hat with "Kansas Safe Hunter" printed on the front when he was shot by fellow safety expert, Gene Brehm. The incident took place just outside a town called Pratt.

A KEY RULE when hunting has to be never look or sound like a game animal, but it is broken with monotonous regularity. Dimitris Thomasinas was hunting ducks in Salonika by hiding and making duck calls, and was killed by another hunter who thought he was the real thing. Endre Bascany imitated a stag's love cry while stalking in Hungary and was also shot, although he survived to tell the tale.

I Spoke Too Soon

Making an emphatic statement about anything is always a risk, you could well be proved wrong. For some people the proof is all too swift and cruel.

WHEN VISITING PARIS in 1931, the author Arnold Bennett, best known for his "Clayhanger" novels, decided to prove to friends that the water there was safe to drink by downing a glass himself. He contracted a fatal dose of typhoid from it and died.

OVERCONFIDENCE in the face of death also did for Kurt Jarlsson of Stockholm. Menaced for years by a recurring nightmare that he would die before he reached 50, he decided to celebrate his survival to the fateful age by throwing a massive celebratory party for friends and relations. To rub home his triumphal escape he dressed up as the Grim Reaper for the occasion, but on leaving his flat to go to the party he accidentally fell seven floors to the ground and was killed instantly.

WILHELM KLIENBERG also found his celebratory party had been scheduled a little too early (or perhaps too late, depending on how you look at it). He was a truck driver for whom his employers threw a party to celebrate his scarcely believable 50 years of accident-free driving. You guessed it – he crashed on the way to the party.

SAFE DRIVING also got school bus driver Lillie Baltrip into serious trouble. Given a safe driving award, she was *en route* to the acceptance ceremony driving a bus containing 29 other school bus drivers when she turned a corner too sharply and overturned. Baltrip and 16 of her passengers were taken to hospital after the accident, but according to Larry Yawn, spokesman for the Houston Independent School District, no one were seriously injured.

AFTER 47 YEARS of accident-free motoring, Parisian Andre Piegue decided to keep this record unblemished by giving up driving at the age of 84. He told his 69-year-old wife Paula, "From now on, you are the family chauffeur," and bought her a new car. On the day it arrived, Paula drove them off to do some shopping, but in the car park she left the car on the slant and Andre, a very fastidious man, could not resist straightening it up. He slid behind the wheel and started it up but, having driven an automatic for years, forgot the new car was manual, with three pedals, not two. As the car eased into place he pressed his right foot down to brake – and hit the accelerator. The car leapt forward, smashed through a hedge, shot across a road, mounted the pavement and crushed a pedestrian – his wife Paula.

FROM THE ASSEMBLED evidence it would seem deeply unwise to celebrate an accident-free anything. In September

1987 the manager of High Marnham power station on the River Trent decreed a special flag should be flown to mark the 100th accident-free day. "Our best effort for years," he said. A security guard was hoisting the flag when the pulley wheel clattered down twenty feet and hit him on the head.

THE SAN ANTONIO Professional Fire-fighters Association staged the 3rd Annual Bush's Canned Foods South Texas Menuendo Cookoff on 17 March 1991, to benefit families whose homes had been destroyed by fire, many of whom were among the 8,000 attending. While the assembled multitude partied, dry grass in the parking lot caught fire and 97 vehicles were destroyed.

THE HICKS FAMILY from Sutton Bridge in Lincolnshire were all set to compete in the 1993 final of the Weight Watchers competition for the healthiest family in Britain, but their hopes were dashed when the whole lot of them went down with 'flu two days before the event was scheduled to take place.

LABOUR MP Rhodri Morgan appeared on BBC Radio Wales to claim that Britain had the world's best electricity supply, explaining that we did not suffer from regular blackouts like many other countries. In mid-flow he was cut off by a short in the transformer room which took the station off the air for 30 seconds.

FRIDAY THE 13TH lived up to its reputation for former airline officer Peter Reyn-Bardt. On that day in May 1983 a man excavating peat in Lindlow Moss, a bog in Cheshire, found a skull with hairs adhering to it and one eyeball still intact, 300 yards from a cottage where Reyn-Bardt had been living when his wife Malika disappeared in 1961. Reyn-Bardt was a homosexual and had married in 1959 to gain respectability with the airline, but the marriage collapsed later that year. In June 1961 his wife returned, demanding cash or she would expose his homosexuality to his employers and was never seen again. When Reyn-Bardt was interviewed by police in January 1983 (why they waited over 20 years is not clear) he said he'd given her £15 and she'd left. Initial tests on the skull revealed it belonged to a European woman aged between 30 and 50 and had been buried for between 5 and 50 years. Confronted with the skull in June 1983, Reyn-Bardt broke down and confessed that he had-strangled Malika, cut her up and buried the pieces near the cottage. However, further tests were done on the skull by an archaeological research lab in Oxford and when these were completed it turned out to be from someone who had died around 410AD, just as the Roman legions were leaving the area. This nonwithstanding, Reyn-Bardt went on trial in Chester in December, his plea of innocence was rejected and he was sentenced to life imprisonment. No trace of his wife has ever been found.

WANDA ENNIS held up a petrol station in Shreveport, Louisiana in 1981. The following day while on a shopping spree, she caught sight of a TV news item which showed a woman robbing the petrol station. Thinking that a hidden camera had caught her in the act, she went to the police and confessed. She should have looked more closely: the film was a reconstruction using a policewoman.

KIM MOLITO is another criminal who should have kept his mouth shut. On trial for burglary in San Antonio, Texas, he objected strongly to the seven-year sentence he was handed down in 1992. Seven, he said, was his unlucky number. The judge sympathised with his problem – and increased the sentence to eight years.

MORTGAGES are a millstone round everyone's neck, so it is easy to sympathise with Ianni and Anna Deluca who had scrimped and saved for 30 years to pay their mortgage on a house in the Milan suburbs. After the last payment they threw a party where they hurled their mortgage papers on the fire, which then got out of control and burnt the house down. They had no insurance: it was one of the corners they'd cut to meet the house payments.

MERRYL BAKER found three teeth in her Galaxy Double Nuts and Raisins chocolate bar. She complained to Mars, the manufacturers, and the story was reported in the Daily Star. Ms. Baker then visited her dentist, where she was told three of her own back teeth were missing. "It was my mistake and I feel such a fool," she said.

CANADIAN GEOLOGIST David Dillon suffered a severe loss of credibility after he positively identified a "meteorite" in Ontario. The piece of supposed space debris turned out to be a giant lump of concrete covered with paint that happened to be standing on a patch of charred grass. "I did get caught up in the whole situation," said the embarassed expert.

OTHER EXPERTS who should have been more careful in their pronouncements include Peter Brown and Julio Riviera. Brown, a snake expert was giving an interview to the BBC in a reptile house when he tweaked the tail of a poisonous adder to prove they were perfectly safe. The snake responded by biting him on the hand. As he fell back, blood pouring from his injury, he gasped, "Don't panic!" and was rushed to Southampton hospital for an antidote.

Lieutenant Colonel Riviera was the military officer in charge of security at the US Embassy in El Salvador when he attempted to demonstrate that a grenade he had found was only a toy. He pulled the pin from it and was killed in the blast.

THE OWNER OF A BLOCK OF FLATS in Grythyttan, Sweden, Kurt Svensson, complained to the board of health about the large number of feral cats in the neighbourhood. As a result about ten cats were shot dead by police. The following day a 41-year-old local man noticed his cat, Knorre, was missing and, assuming that Svennson was responsible for its death, hurled abuse at him and threatened to kill him. That evening, Svensson's block of flats burned down, making him and four other families homeless. The fire was proved to be arson and witnesses reported seeing the cat-owner fleeing the scene. He was tried, found guilty and sentenced to eight years imprisonment. However, on returning home after his crime, he had found the missing cat asleep in his living room. If no one offered to look after the cat while he was in prison, though, it would be put down.

Wrong End of the Stick

Misunderstandings are easily made, some with dramatic consequences.

ACTOR Luther Charles, out of work and desperate for a part, cut off both his ears when he saw an ad for a musical which wanted "Genuine earless performers". But when he showed up at the Ohio theatre, the show's producers were appalled – the ad was a misprint and what they actually wanted was *fearless* actors. Although Charles's actions showed a degree of fearlessness as well, he still failed to get the part; he got psychiatric treatment instead.

WHEN INTERFLORA sent out a "Say it with flowers" campaign mailshot to hundreds of families at Christmas 1994, they accidentally targeted people who had died the previous year. A list of those who had died was fed into the computer organising the sales drive instead of being used to remove them from the company's mailing lists. Bereavement counsellors had to be brought in to deal with protests from hundreds of grieving families and to comfort distraught sales staff who were having to bear the brunt of the complaints.

UNABLE to bear the thought of his ex-wife Rosa living with another man, even after their divorce, Isaac Gutierrez became jealous when he phoned her one day and heard what he thought was a man's voice in the background. Arming himself with a gun he charged round to Rosa's house, broke in and shot dead the bearded stranger who confronted him. It was Catherine Lankford, a "bearded lady" who occasionally worked in the circus and was a friend of his wife. In Milan another jealous husband, convinced his wife had left him for another man, shot her and her sister dead – then found they had just been out shopping together.

NEW MUM Irene Copeland of West Virginia, came home to find a toothbrush with lipstick on it in their bathroom and caused £10,000 of damage to the house before her husband could explain that it belonged to his mother. Another suspicious wife, Connie Baker burst into a house in Houston, Texas, believing her husband was there with another woman, and was shot dead by the owner, a total stranger.

ALSO A VICTIM of mistaken identity was Jonathan Hicks, aged 3. He was enthralled by the lights on the family Christmas tree and crept downstairs in the middle of the night to look at them. The family home, in the crime-riddled area of West Jackson, Mississippi, was a virtual fortress, and as Jonathan entered the living room he set off an anti-crime motion detector alerting his stepmother to intruders. She grabbed a .38-calibre handgun, rushed downstairs and shot at the first movement she saw, killing the boy instantly.

A JAPANESE MOTORIST, seeing a man dash out of a shop wielding a knife, took prompt action and ran him over. The robber, however, turned out to be a Tokyo policeman taking part in a crime-prevention drill.

82-YEAR-OLD New Zealander Richard Morsted was arrested for seeking sex from prostitutes in Auckland and spent a night in prison before he could persuade them that he had a facial spasm. His twitch causes him to nod and wink convulsively, and the police had interpreted it as an attempt to catch the attention of a prostitute.

A SLAUGHTERMAN in Victoria, Australia was told to collect a cow, but went to the wrong paddock and shot dead a prize-winning racehorse instead.

STEVE LAWRENCE knelt down beside a busy road to coax a hedgehog out of the way of traffic – and was promptly arrested for suspected burglary when suspicious neighbours saw his crouching figure and called the police.

APPRENTICE MOHEL Yitzhak Nagar went knocking on doors in an immigrant neighbourhood in Beersheba, Israel, seeking baby boys in need of his services as a rabbi who performs circumcisions under Jewish law. When he knocked on the door of Irna Pundersky, a recent immigrant from Russia who spoke little Hebrew, Nagar thought he had found a client because when she held up her son for examination he could see he was not circumcised, so he fetched his colleague Shlomo Maman to carry out the operation. When they returned they asked Mrs Pundersky to leave the room as they did not want to upset her, and set about circumcising the boy. When she returned she was distraught at what she saw and filed a kidnapping complaint with the police, who investigated, along with the Religious Ministry. They found that although no laws had been broken, neither Nagar or Maman held a licence to practise circumcision. The men were accused of bungling their duties because the baby lacked a crucial precondition for religious circumcision – he was not Jewish.

GUARDS AT HEATHROW airport called in the bomb squad when they found what they thought was a ring of plastic explosive wrapped round a woman's waist. When they extracted the suspicious package, it turned out to be a length of spicy Italian sausage.

AFTER ATTENDING A SALE organised by Universal Trader Ltd of Elstree, Eric Duffield believed he had been suckered into paying £80 for a camera and two watches he did not want, so he confronted the salesmen. One of them saw wires attached to Eric's belt and ripped them off, accusing him of being a plant who was recording their sales patter and transmitting it to someone outside. The wires, however, belonged to a pain-killing device which allows Eric to control the pain of a damaged spine with electronic signals.

COASTGUARDS on the Firth of Forth watched but did nothing as flares and fires lit up the small island of Inchkeith on Halloween 1992. Only after further reports were received was the Kinghorn lifeboat was finally sent out. The flares were in fact SOS signals from William and George Redpath, whose 21ft yacht was badly holed on rocks after developing engine trouble. The coastguards thought the fires and lights were part of some weird ritual, a spokesman said. "The island is supposed to be connected with witchcraft."

AN ELDERLY WOMAN in Bristol set her house on fire and ended up in hospital being treated for smoke inhalation after she struck a match and lit the top of her new log-effect electric fire, confused by the log's realistic appearance.

GOING FISHING with his 16-year-old grandson, Sven Harkus set out from the town of Sundsvall on central Sweden's rolling plains for a 60-mile trip to the Jamtland lakes. On the way home he turned north instead of south and, despite regularly asking directions, ended up three days later 900 miles away in the Norwegian town of Kirkenes, near the Russian border. Their journey finally came to an end when Harkus fell asleep at the wheel and crashed into a ditch. Possibly confused by the 24-hour sunlight, both were convinced they were still near Sundvall, despite Norway's dramatic fjords and mountains. When police told them where they were, they had to be treated for shock. A relative was expected to come and collect them. Police said they hoped he was a better map-reader.

POP STAR Lena Fiagbe also got lost when trying to appear on the Radio One roadshow in Bangor. She wandered confused around the North Wales town, only to find the party was actually going on in Bangor, Northern Ireland. To add insult to injury, she had flown in from Ireland the day before specially for the event. She missed the chance to perform her hit single "Got to Get it Right".

TAKE THAT were the downfall of Isle of Wight Tory councillor John Wooldridge. He booked the band to play at his nightclub Booker T's in Newport, and splashed out £2,000 on a champagne reception for them, wrote out VIP invites for the performance, had hundreds of posters print-

ed and took on 20 extra bouncers to cope with the antici-
pated teenage horde. The only problem was that the band
he had booked was, in fact, Fake That, a local band of Take
That impersonators consisting of a welder, a computer consultant, a holiday camp redcoat, a carpenter and a barman
doing their first gig. Nigel Smith, who had booked the band,
was surprised to be asked to lay on such lavish treatment by
Mr Wooldridge, but said, "He's the boss and I do what he
says." Mr Wooldridge said, "Nigel rang me one night. The
pub was noisy, but I'm sure he said he had booked Take
That." He still believed he was getting the real band when
he met the group and it was only when he asked which one
was Robbie and they all raised their hands that he twigged
something was wrong.

SANDRA ROBERTSON waited all day for the green carpet she'd chosen for her home in Hardwick Place, Woburn
Sands, Buckinghamshire. Eventually she called Allied
Carpets, who called the freelance fitter on his mobile just as
he was putting the finishing touches to the carpet in a bungalow with the same number in nearby Hardwick Road.
He'd been let into the empty property by an electrician who
was working there. By coincidence, the front room at the
bungalow had been cleared of furniture, so the fitter had set
to work.

Stuck!

**It seems that if you can get caught in it,
someone will get caught in it.**

IN MALMO, Sweden, a pensioner fell foul of her seating in 1989. As the 80-year-old woman sat down to sunbathe on her balcony, her deck-chair fabric tore and the chair folded up, leaving her with her head trapped between her knees. She remained there for 48 hours until a caretaker across the street noticed her sitting in a peculiar fashion and called the police.

GRANT SHITTIT, an unfortunately named resident of Timaru, New Zealand, was making his way home after a night on the tiles when he decided he needed to lie down, choosing a bed of "lovely soft moss" for the purpose. However, on waking up the next day, he found he had been mistaken, and the "moss" was actually wet cement which had dried overnight, leaving him stuck fast with only his head free. Despite his screams, he remained there for 72 hours until a passing motorist mistook his head for an injured hedgehog and stopped. He was freed by firemen with pneumatic drills. Commenting on his ordeal he apparently said, "It was particularly uncomfortable because I'd been sick on myself in the night."

AA RESCUE VEHICLES spent eight hours battling to extract Paul Rudd's van from a mudpatch. At 3pm a relay truck sent to free the van was sucked into the mud beside it. Two hours later a 15-ton truck arrived to get them both out, but it also became wedged, jamming both the relay truck and Mr Rudd's van in. A 38-tonner got stuck too, at which point Mr. Rudd gave up and got a lift home. It took until the next morning to free all the vehicles.

A WYLTHENSHAWE man entered a phonebox in June 1994 while somewhat the worse for wear, then realised he couldn't remember how he had got in. He tried pushing each side in turn, but could not find the door. In a panic he dialled 999 and a fire crew duly arrived, to find him slumped to the floor from his efforts. Swiftly sizing up the situation, one fireman stepped forward and held the door open, letting the prisoner stumble off into the night. A similar fate befell a Swindon cyclist. As he made a call, his bike fell against the phonebox door, wedging it shut, also necessitating a 999 call to regain his freedom.

STREET FURNITURE of a different kind caused problems in Wrexham, Clwyd. A late-night stroller through the town was amazed to hear cries for help from a post box outside the sorting office in Regent's Street. A middle-aged postman had been collecting late deliveries 20 minutes earlier when a gust of wind blew the door shut behind him. Another GPO worker had been trapped in the same box 25 years earlier.

A FRENCHMAN who understandably wished to remain anonymous tried to buy a condom at one in the morning in Briec de l'Odet, Brittany, and got his hand jammed in the machine. Four hours later a group of teenagers found him, but couldn't persuade the fire brigade to take their story seriously. Eventually police coaxed the firemen out, and they cut the man free and took him to hospital.

IT IS NOT JUST CONDOM MACHINES which seem to have developed predatory instincts. In Gravesend, Kent, the fire brigade had to be called out to rescue a gambler from a fruit machine which had grabbed his fingers as he tried to collect his winnings. In Southampton a Coke machine turned nasty. A 22-year-old undergraduate, named only as Fiona, tried to buy a Coke from a vending machine in the chemistry department foyer, but no can appeared in the slot, so she tried to encourage it and became trapped up to her shoulder. Friends and staff tried to free her for 20 minutes, then called the fire brigade. To work out what to do, they first dismantled another machine, then, with an ambulance crew administering pain-killers to Fiona, they went to work on the real thing. When she was finally released, suffering only mild bruising, Fiona at least left clutching her can.

TOILETS TURNED nasty in Stockholm when a badly decomposed body of a young man was found in a doctor's waiting room toilet there. Police said he had been there for two months while the loo was locked for rebuilding work. Elsewhere, toilet victims have been more lucky. Paul Massey of Erith in Kent was freed from his toilet after getting his leg immovably wedged in it while trying to stamp on a spider crawling along the seat. In France one unfortunate had to be stretchered away from a high-speed train with a sawn-off toilet bowl wrapped round his wrist in full view of TV news cameras. He had become stuck while trying to retrieve his wallet from the S-bend.

DE WITT FINLEY got stuck in the snow in autumn 1994 while trying to drive the back roads over the Klamath Mountains in the US. Being a religious man, he put his faith in God and waited for him to send someone to rescue him. He sat there for 9 weeks, checking off the days on his salesman's year planner and writing a stack of letters to his two sons, his fiancée and his boss, until sometime around 19 January 1995 he finally starved to death. It was not until May when his pick-up was finally found by a group of teenagers who themselves had got stuck and were *en route* for help. Finley showed no sign of ever having left his vehicle. If he had, he would have found that a few yards round the corner there was clear road leading down the mountain to safety.

AUSTRALIAN Laura McKenzie also showed an amazing reluctance to leave her vehicle in the face of problems. She stopped her car at a red light – and stayed there for 2 days waiting for it to change. "How was I supposed to know it was broken? It was red so I just behaved properly," she said from hospital where she was being treated for dehydration.

NEW YORK COP Levett Sponge saw a bank raid in progress and rushed in through the bank's revolving doors to intervene. Unfortunately the 23-stone Sponge was more than the door could handle and it jammed with him inside it. When the robbers stopped laughing they realised the revolving door was the only way out of the bank, and after frantic attempts to dislodge the portly cop, they gave themselves up. In Derby, Lee Smith, 20, spent 8 hours in a revolving door at a supermarket when the automatic lock activated as he passed through. Workmates were forced to wait until the next morning before they could get a key to free him.

EVERY SO OFTEN an incident occurs which justifies one of those so-called irrational fears. This was the case with the experience of Moira Poor, 69, who entered a lift at the Auckland City Council car park in New Zealand on the afternoon of Friday 9 December 1994 and was trapped when it stuck between floors. The emergency alarm didn't work because the batteries were flat, and there was no telephone. Mrs Poor was carrying nothing but her handbag. She was not found for the entire weekend, which she spent sleeping on the floor, or standing yelling for help. On Monday morning, after 67 hours, she was finally discovered and freed. Going to her car to drive out, she had to present her expired parking ticket at the pay booth, where the attendant refused to believe her explanation and forced her to pay an excess charge, then told her she stank and should be ashamed of herself. A few days later, though, the city council awarded her £2,100 and free parking in Auckland for life.

FIRE OFFICERS from Rotherham's Red Watch carried out a safety drill on how to rescue people stuck in a lift at the Beversleigh flats in the town. The 11 firemen and the flat's caretaker piled into the lift – only to become hopelessly stuck between floors. They had no choice but to sound the alarm, which attracted the attention of a resident who told them she'd go and get a caretaker. He explained he was already in there, so she said she'd call the fire brigade instead, "We are the Fire Brigade!" chorused the trapped officers. In the end they all had to be rescued by another team from the neighbouring Darnell fire station.

TEN POLICE AND FIRE OFFICERS answered the emergency call from Sara Rolfe in Bracknell, Berkshire. Dressed in a black basque and stockings she had demanded her partner Chris Portis handcuff her to the bed for sex, but when he came to free her, the key broke off in the lock. They had trouble convincing the emergency operator their call was genuine, but once she had stopped laughing, the alert brought a massive response. The horde of emergency workers filled the flat, laughing, while Sara was freed with bolt cutters.

THREE OLD LADIES from Leipzig, Germany, took a sauna together at the house of Elfriede Kreuger, 68 and became trapped when a faulty door handle jammed. Elfriede and her two friends aged 62 and 71 were locked in from lunch until tea when her brother, worried because she had missed a hairdressing appointment, went round and broke the door down. By that time, though, all three had died of heart attacks brought on by the 125°C heat.

KENNETH McLAUGHLIN was planting chrysanthemums on his mother's grave when he became trapped as the ground gave way, leaving him stuck up to his knees in soft ground around the base of the headstone. He remained that way for two hours until help arrived.

CHAPTER EIGHTEEN

Surprise!

Disasters happen when you least expect them.

LOVERS Anna Malerba, 23, and Mario Franco, 25, were hit by lightning and badly burned as they had sex in a field in Bolzano, Italy. In Japan, golfer Kano Yashamura was hit and killed by a 220-yard drive which struck him on the head. The ball bounced off, straight into the hole – a hole in one.

TWO STUDENTS from the University of Chicago were walking down an alley in the city when they were hit on the head by a flying dishwasher. The landlord of the building they were passing hurled it out the window onto a garbage heap and did not notice they were passing. In Irving Township, New Jersey, Joseph Frankor, 45, ended up trapped in his car for 20 minutes after someone committed suicide by leaping off an overpass onto the vehicle, crushing it and wedging Frankor inside.

CHAPTER EIGHTEEN

IN OAKHAM, Leicestershire, a man was caught short when the portable toilet he was using was hoisted in the air by a forklift truck while he was still inside with his trousers round his ankles. He was luckier than a Venezuelan youth who was stricken with diarrhoea while visiting the zoo. 19-year-old Alexander Perez jumped over a wall to answer the call of nature in some bushes, but, he recalled, "I had my trousers around my knees when I heard some growling and saw this ferocious animal hurling itself on top of me." He wrestled frantically with the lioness whose enclosure he'd picked to dump in, trying to pull his trousers up as she sank her claws and teeth into his head and torso. He was rescued after a friend knocked the lioness out with a brick.

A TOURIST who collapsed on a trip round Buckingham Palace had a surprise when he woke up after being flown home in an air ambulance – he was in Santiago, Chile. The only problem was that the 40-year-old patient came from Santiago, Spain, which is 740 miles from London, not 7,000. 151 Chinese men received a similar unwelcome shock. They stowed away on a cargo ship in Asia, aiming to make it to the US to make their fortunes. Unfortunately they landed in Haiti, the poorest country in the western hemisphere instead.

SUSPECTED DIAMOND SMUGGLER Phil McLean was under orders not to leave Gambia, while a court decided whether he should pay a £200,000 fine or serve six years in gaol for smuggling. This, however did not stop Weymouth and Portland District Council sending him a poll-tax demand. They put the bill for £309.99 in the diplomatic bag to the British Embassy in the Gambian capital, Banjul, and officials there traced him to a village 15 miles away. Mr

McLean said, "This is all I need. As if I haven't got enough to worry about, I only lived in Weymouth for a couple of months back in 1991." His girlfriend, Lyn Cummings, blamed a local witchdoctor whom she said had put the couple under a curse: "He spends all his time chanting in the village and dancing naked round cow horns," she said. "Every day we have had people outside casting spells, it's been a nightmare." Weymouth Council said, "We are obliged to pursue debts."

MOTORIST Nicola Ratcliffe received a parking ticket after workmen painted yellow lines under her car while it was parked overnight. Contractors carefully lifted her car out the way as they painted the lines late one night outside Nicola's home near Newmarket in Suffolk, then put it back. At 2am a passing policeman noticed the vehicle on the newly painted lines and issued a £20 ticket. "When I moved the car I realised they must have lifted it up and moved it to paint the lines underneath because there was no gap where the tyres had been," she said. She appealed against her fine and the ticket was cancelled.

A CAR HIRE firm in Canterbury, got a surprise when they discovered the fate of one of its missing cars. Steve Smith of S&B Car Hire discovered that a second-hand Ford Fiesta, which had been hired out to Ian Leitch in January 1993, had been destroyed by rocket fire – not a usual occurrence in a peaceful cathedral city. However, after hiring the car, Leitch had headed off to Bosnia in it, where it was pressed into service as a field ambulance and eventually blasted by Serbs.

PENSIONER Yvonne Martin, who had grown up in a convent orphanage, tried to trace the family she never knew, and found out that she did not exist. She placed a newspaper ad under her original name, Joan Martin, and giving her date of birth in the hope of locating lost relatives. Instead she turned up another Joan Martin, who was born in the same hospital on the same day to the same parents, and had an identical birth certificate, plus the family history to authenticate it. All this has left Yvonne totally baffled. Now she has no idea of who she was, or when and where she was born. "It seems I don't have a past at all," she said.

A MARRIED MAN and his lover, also married but to someone else, sloped off for a romantic evening in a holiday cottage near their homes in Shoumen, north-east Bulgaria. Hearing lively music from a nearby house they took some wine and went to join the party. Inside they found their own partners locked in a passionate embrace. The wives hurled themselves at each other and began to fight furiously, with their husbands only intervening when they set about each other with garden hoes. Once they'd managed to subdue the women the two husbands accompanied their own wives home amid cheers from the crowd which had been drawn by the rumpus.

POLICE IN UTAH raced round to a house after a baby accidentally dialled the emergency number. Bursting through the door, they found the child's father with a large hoard of cocaine.

Similarly, when Orlando Jaramillio was stopped for driving the wrong way down a one-way street, his odd behaviour prompted police to search his car. They found a satchel containing $300,000 which he was unable to explain convincingly. Police then got a search warrant for his house, where they turned up another $4.7 million of suspected drug money hidden behind a false wall.

CLEARING out his basement in Westminster, Vermont, Tom Hutchins came across some crates left by the previous owner of the house, a pilot. Two days later, as he mowed the lawn, he idly wondered why there were so many planes circling overhead. Then his lawn started to fill with men in combat fatigues with radios. It turned out that when he moved one of the crates in his basement, he had unwittingly activated an aircraft distress beacon stored inside it. This caused more than a hundred rescuers from the Air Force and other agencies to be scrambled to track down the "crash". Their direction-finders led them to Hutchins's basement, where they switched the beacon off.

THIS TALE FROM the Pacific coast of the Soviet Union is almost certainly an urban legend, but still bears repeating. A capsized boat was found drifting out at sea with only one survivor clinging to the wreckage. When rescued he explained that the boat had been wrecked by a cow falling into it from the sky. The authorities declined to believe his story, and sent him to a mental hospital for his pains. Nevertheless he stuck to his tale, so the authorities decided to investigate. They discovered that on the day in question an aircraft about to fly from a local airstrip had been delayed by a cow grazing on the runway. The crew, worrying about food shortages like everyone else, decided to take it with them. They drove it into the plane via the bomb bay and took off. All was well until they reached cruising height, where the cold made the cow agitated. Fearing for the plane's safety, the crew jettisoned her over the sea, where she landed on the unfortunate fisherman's boat and sank it.

MARION FERGUSSON, 42, was walking past the offices

of Swinton Insurance in Ormskirk, when a heavy sign advertising accident insurance fell on her, breaking four ribs and
cutting her head. She needed eight stitches in the head
wound and three weeks in hospital, but was awarded £6,800
compensation.

Hell on Wheels

If guns are the riskiest things to let people loose with, cars come a close second.

EUGENIUS WIMPLE, a Zimbabwean golfer, became highly excited after scoring a hole in one, leapt into his golf buggy and careered euphorically around the course. Later, a fellow player explained, "He didn't see the toilet because it was hidden behind a hummock. He just flew over the hump, screamed, 'Christ, a bog,' and crashed straight into it." Four people were using the makeshift bamboo toilet at the time and two of them were seriously injured. One of the victims said, "One minute I was on the loo, the next I was straddling a golf buggy. Next time I'll go in the bushes."

A BEACH BUGGY rather than a golf buggy was Hilda Wilson's nemesis. Hilda, 59, had saved up for a break in Florida to get away from her Belfast home for a while, but no sooner did she get there than she had a run-in with the two-ton buggy. She was dozing on the beach when she heard someone yell, but it was too late. The heavy vehicle drove straight across her chest, crushing her ribs and puncturing her lungs. Lifeguard Catherine Cleary said, "The front tyre must have missed her head by inches."

HARRY DALE, 62, of Hunstanton, Norfolk, dreamed that thieves stole the roof-rack from his car, so the next day he removed it for safe-keeping. Someone stole his car instead.

TO PROTECT his 15-year-old Opel Kadett, Andrew Roddison removed his high-tension ignition lead, fixed a double-lock steering bar, set an electronic immobiliser and locked the doors and the boot. Nonetheless the rusting banger, bought for £200, was still stolen five times in under a fortnight. Roddison, aged 19, from Sheffield, said, "I am told I might now be the owner of Britain's most stolen car, but it's no fun. I'm sick with worry, and baffled. How do thieves do it?" His stepfather suspected someone was doing it as a joke, but police ruled this out because the Opel had been taken from a succession of different places.

RICHARD WESTON from Nottingham was perhaps even more unlucky with his stolen car. As he left the police station where he had reported its theft, he was run over by his own car. Fortunately he was only slightly injured. Good Samaritan Pierre Morache also had problems with his car being stolen. He helped three youths push-start a car in Carcassonne, France, but did not realise it was his car they were starting until it was disappearing down the road.

A CAR doesn't need to be stolen to run its owner over. William Kay, 73, stopped to buy a paper in Sunrise, Florida, and left his car idling. As he walked behind it the automatic transmission slipped from "park" into "reverse" and the vehicle started moving, running him down as it did so. Not content with flattening him once, the car continued to run backwards in tight circles, running over Kay on each circuit, making 10 in all. Bystander Meyer Barber suffered cuts and bruises as he tried to snatch the ignition key from the driverless vehicle, but to no avail. Kay was dead before the ambulance reached him.

IT'S NOT JUST CARS that circle maliciously to run people down either. Edward Flewitt, 26, came to grief when the outboard motor on his speedboat stalled and he pulled the cord to restart it. The motor had been left in gear and fired with a jerk, throwing Flewitt overboard, leaving the boat running in circles out of control. As he struggled in the water, the 15ft craft circled round and struck Flewitt on the head knocking him unconscious and drowning him. Inspector John Dawson of Newport, Isle of Wight, said, "It is normal for boats to go round in circles if left to themselves, but I've never heard of an accident like this."

AN ALL-GIRL choir of German yodellers narrowly avoided a serious accident after they caused their coach driver to have a heart attack by making too much noise. The driver had made several pleas for quiet, but the girls just kept on yodelling until he collapsed, causing the bus to hit a crash barrier. A passenger steered the bus to safety and the driver recovered in hospital.

Norma Steven of Penarth, Wales, did not suffer a heart attack, but still lost control of her car after a spider dangled in front of her, suspended from her sun visor, while she drove. As she panicked, her car veered into a parked Ford, writing it off and causing £1,500 of damage to her own car. Mrs Steven was hospitalised with a broken breastbone.

ON CHRISTMAS DAY 1994, bus driver Niyi Owoeye was driving near Akure, capital of Nigeria's Ondo state, when he saw an antelope at the side of the road, and decided to run it over. It was only after he had crushed it that he discovered the "antelope" was in fact Mr Ratimi Alesanmi, a member of the Federal Commission for Road Safety.

STONINGTON LOBSTER CO-OPERATIVE of Maine, USA, lost one of their trucks in a serious accident on a Connecticut highway. The vehicle overturned, leaving the driver pinned and bleeding in the wreckage. As paramedics worked to free the driver, fire-fighters helped themselves to his load of lobsters, despite his weak protests. The driver's foot had to be amputated as a result of the crash, and the co-operative's manager made a complaint to Joe Benoit, the local fire chief. When asked what had happened to the lobsters, Benoit replied, "They took them back to the firehouse and had a feed." He offered to pay for the crustaceans, but his offer was refused and the co-op continued to press their complaint.

FRANK AND MARIE MOOR of Bournemouth, Dorset, set off for a caravanning holiday in France, only they forgot the caravan. The blunder was spotted by their son who saw it in their garden shortly after waving goodbye to them. The couple finally realised their error when a local radio station broadcast a message advising them to look in their rear-view mirror.

A LORRY DRIVER on the M1 was startled when two huge

wheels overtook him and crashed down an embankment just outside Sheffield. He pulled over to investigate and found they had come off his own potato lorry.

A VANITY PLATE gave retired police chief Robert Temple a good deal more than a distinctive registration number – it also brought him $100,000 worth of parking tickets. The situation arose because Temple, who had not driven in New York for 12 years, had acquired a registration plate reading "Temp", his nickname on the force. The problem is that TEMP is an abbreviation used in New York City for parking tickets written out to vehicles with temporary registration stickers. Unfortunately, when put through the traffic computer, it came up with Temple's address and sent him all the tickets.

The situation was finally resolved, but not permanently, for two years later the same thing happened to Claire Hurd of Locust, New Jersey. Hurd worked regularly for office temping agencies and also had a licence plate reading "Temp", and so she too became the target of a deluge of tickets, this time from New Jersey and Pennsylvania as well as New York. When she raised the matter with New York officials they told her the problem was entirely her fault as the plates were "bad", but they did eventually apologise.

RUSSIAN KGB bosses attempting retrieve funds that had been secreted around Europe by agents during the Cold War, got a surprise when they tried to get back £140,000 stashed in France – the Grenoble-Lyon motorway had been built over it.

A POLICE road-safety display bus was put out of action after a pile-up. While *en route* to a gala the bus was in collision with a 17-ton lorry, another bus, a motorbike and a car. The bus was left with a smashed windscreen, a buckled front and a scrape down the side, while the driver suffered a sprained wrist. The show in Earlsheaton, West Yorkshire, was called off. "We could hardly take along a damaged vehicle," said a police spokesman.

SCHOOLTEACHER Timothy Bode, 39, stopped his car and went to protest to a driver that she might have killed him by pulling out in front of him. As he did so he was struck and killed by a car driven by Lucy Dolling, 79. Woodrow Kreekmore fared no better, he narrowly escaped death when his car skidded off an icy road and slammed into a telegraph pole outside Chickasha, Oklahoma. Unhurt, he climbed out and strolled into the road to hitch a lift. He had only gone a couple of feet when the telegraph pole keeled over and struck him dead. David Fuller of Winchester met a similar fate: he survived a crash on the central reservation of the A31, only to be mown down by an articulated truck as he stepped from his car to cross the busy road to safety.

References

REFERENCES

CHAPTER 1: WHY BOTHER?

Pole *D.Record* 15 May 1992. Mountain *Independent* 19 Dec 1986. Suicide *Houston Post* 13 Sept 1990. Move *International Herald Tribune* 20 Jul 1992. Gun *Victoria (B.C.) Times-Colonist* 19 Sept 1990. Armed robber *D.Mirror* 28 Sept 1995. Family Tree *Western Morning News* 28 Apr 1994. Bears *Independent* 26 Jul 1995. Heavy Metal *Big Issue* 20 Feb 1995. Clock *D.Mirror* 2 Jun 1993, *Edinburgh Eve. News* 12 Jan 1990. *News of the World* 21 Aug 1988, *Sussex Eve. Argus* 20 Dec 1993. Security *D.Mirror* 25 May 1990, *D.Telegraph* 16 Sept 1986, *Reuters* 20 Jul 1994. Lonely Heart *Chesterfield & Dronfield Gazette* 20 May 1988, *News of the World* 15 Dec 1991. Cicciolina *Guardian* 26 Apr 1989. Seal *Observer* 4 Oct 1992. Plant *D. Telegraph* 18 Nov 1988. Fireman *D.Telegraph* 25 Jul 1986. HWP *D.Telegraph* 23 Aug 1986. Eiffel *D.Record* 18 Mar 1996.

CHAPTER 2: NAME OF THE BEAST

Pitbull *Halifax Eve Courier* 12 Aug 1994. Scrappy *Eve. Times* Dec 1993. Leg *News of the World* 18 Mar 1990. Tongue *Edinburgh Eve. News* 14 Oct 1993. Dog Drivers *Hartford Courant* 28 Jul 1993, *S.Express* 15 Jun 1980. Gundogs *S.Mirror* 3 Aug 1975, *D.Telegraph* 4 Aug 1982. Rabbit *The People* 20 Nov 1994. Revenge *AP* Date unknown, *D.Telegraph* 21 Dec 1987, *D.Mail* 19 Nov 1991, *Reuters* 16 Dec 1995, *Houston Chronicle* 9 Jul 1996. Pig *The News* 17 Feb 1988. Frog blast *S.Mail* 21 Mar 1993. Flies *Sun* 22 Jul 1988. Roo *The Times* 18 Oct 1986. Ass *S.Mail* 8 Nov 1992. Cow *The Sun* 9 Apr 1993. Electrocution *D.Mail* 10 Jan 1995. Potoroos *D.Telegraph* 18 Feb 1993. Big birds *Eve. Leader* 8 Jan 1992. Cowpat *Northern Echo* May 1993. Bird Eats *Today* 9 Oct 1991, *D.Telegraph* 9 Oct 1991, *Hull D.Mail* 24 Jan 1990, *Bristol Eve. Post* 17 Oct 1990. Radiator *The Sun* 13 Apr 1989. Tragopan *Johannesburg Star* 24 Jan 1991, *Big Issue* 22-29 Apr 1996. Walrus *The Sun* 7 Apr 1989, *D.Telegraph* 17 Oct 1995. Flat Cat *Big Issue* 15-21 Apr 1996.

CHAPTER 3: ASKING FOR IT

X-ray *D.Star* 21 Aug 1993. Rat Trap *Observer* 11 Oct 1992, *Clwyd & Chester Evening Leader* 16 Mar 1993. Scorpion *Sussex Eve. Argus* 7 Jul 1994, *Edinburgh Eve. News* 26 Feb 1992. Croc *D.Mirror* 13 Oct 1987. Ostrich *S.Express* 22 Mar 1987. Fat *Coventry Eve. Telegraph* 24 Jun 1994. End *Coventry Eve. Telegraph* 5 Sept. 1994. Chastity belt *The People* 12 Jun 1994. Nagging *D.Mirror* 13 Jul 1987. Cash *D.Record* 13 Sept 1994, The Sun 11 Dec 1992. Memory *News of the World* 14 Jul 1991, *D.Mirror* 28 Aug 1992, *New York Post* 10 May 1995. Surgeons *Guardian* 18 Dec 1990. Milk *The Sun* 23 Sept 1992. Healer *D.Telegraph* 2 Oct 1989. Seat belt *Independent* 19 May 1987. Bowling Ball *D.Record* 9 Apr 1994, *Independent* 4 Aug 1987. Cross-country *Atlanta Constitution* 14 May 1992, *The Sun* 12 Jul 1986. Carrot *S.Express* 17 Sept.1995 Package *Independent* 20 Jan 1993. U-Boat *D.Star* 7 Jul 1992.

CHAPTER 4: DAMNED IF YOU DO...

Safari parks *Guardian, D. Mail, Western Morning News* 11 Aug 1994, *D.Telegraph* 8 Aug 1995. Philippou *Toronto Globe and Mail* 27 Jan 1990. Extinguisher *Times of Oman* 19 Jan 1995. Wasps *Europa Times* Dec 1993, *D.Telegraph* 6 Sept 1988. Speed limit *The People* 4 Sept 1994. Exposure *Guardian* 12 Jul 1994. Miracle *Overseas Jobs Express* 1 Oct 1993. Pylon *S.Express* 13 Feb 1983. Stove *D.Star* 19 May 1994. Bag Snatch *D.Telegraph* 13 Oct 1993. Obstetrician *Boston Sunday Globe* 7 Nov 1993. Snakebite *D.Telegraph* 24 Apr 1981, *Dundee Evening Telegraph* 30 May 1990. Farmer *Guardian* 21 Aug 1981.

CHAPTER 5: NOT THEIR DAY

Cibonco Mala *D.Mirror* 18 Jun 1994. Israeli Woman *Jerusalem Post* 25 Aug 1988. Hodgeson *Scotsman* 16 Aug 1990. DIY *Sunday Express* 11 Dec 1994. Fishing *Guardian* 13 Apr 1995. Motorcyclist *News of the World* 29 Jan 1979. Snake *Weekend* 11 Feb 1989. Top Car *D.Telegraph* 24 Aug 1993. Aircraft *Melbourne Age* 16 Dec 1985. Research *Guardian* 7 Dec 1994. Ditert *D.Mirror* 19 Feb 1990. Huang *Bangkhat Post* 16 Jun 1995. Ruiz *S.Express* 18 Jun 1978. Guiholt *Europa Times* Jan 1994. Wedding *D.Star* 24 Feb 1994. Brundall Wedding *Eastern Daily Press* 11 Jul 1994. Filipino *Hong Kong Standard* 31 Jul 1994. Sri Lankans *D.Telegraph* 10 Aug 1990. Classic *St.Catherine's Journal* 14 Mar 1839.

CHAPTER 6: DEAD UNLUCKY

Clover *D.Mirror* 20 Nov 1992. Sex *D.Star* 16 May 1994. House *Independent* 9 Jul 1994. Marker *National Enquirer* 25 Feb 1986. Vancouver *Edinburgh Evening News* 1 Nov 1991. Forgotten corpse *New York Daily News* 20 Jul 1994. Wrong Corpse *New York Daily News* 20 Aug 1988. Returns *National Enquirer* 5 Nov 1991, *D.Mirror* 30 Mar 1992. Sailor *D.Record* 27 Jul 1990. Smoker *D.Mirror* 5 November 1986. Romeo and Juliet *D.Telegraph* 30 Jan 1985. Sick joke *D.Star* 12 Jan 1994. Asset *New York Daily News* 11 Dec 1994. Gravestone *D.Record* 11 Jul 1987.

CHAPTER 7: WRATH OF GOD

Holy Water *D.Telegraph* 18 Feb 1992. Blessings *Guardian* 13 Apr 1982, *Herald Tribune* 23 Nov 1979. Doomsday *D.Star* 17 Nov 1994. Dublin *D.Record* 30 Sept 1993. CruciFiction *City Limits* 3-10 Apr 1986. Teeth *D.Mirror* 22 Jan 1988. Dildo *The Aquarian* 1-8 Apr 1981. Rain prayers *S.Express* 19 Jan 1996, *Europa Times* May 1994. Cross fall *The Sun* 6 Oct 1992. Collapses *Daily Star* 28 Sept. 1994, *The People* 16 January 1994. Soil *Halifax Eve. Courier* 30 May 1995. Hajj *The Independent* 25 May 1994, Independent, *D.Mirror* 12 Jul 1991. Alcohol *The Independent* 16 Apr 1991. Cheque *St.Louis Post-Despatch* 16 Dec 1994. Cement *Independent* 12 Jul 1991. Builder *D.Mirror* 7 Mar 1990. Window *Western Mail* 9 Apr 1994. U.P. God *AP* 15 Feb 1996, *(NY) Press Republican* 1 May 1986.

CHAPTER 8: HEALTH HAZARD

Medical Journal *Guardian* 27 Dec 1988. Light *Sun* 5 Mar 1987. Hands *S.Mail* 18 Apr 1993, *Europa Times* Apr 1994. Penis *Express & Star* 5 Sept 1992. Urine *Belfast Telegraph* 27 Apr 1994. Shoes *Sun* 16 May 1992. Oxygen *Lewiston Sun-Journal* 28 Mar 1994. Braces *People* 2 Jan 1994. Doors *S.Express* 19 Mar 1995, *Guardian* 18 Jan 1995. Old Dupha *Columbia Dispatch* 19 Apr 1990. Respray *D.Mirror* 21 May 1986. Ambulance *AP* 5 Jan 1995. Sanchez *AP* 1&18 Mar 1995, *Coventry Eve. Telegraph* 19 Jul 1995. Ears *D.Mirror* 24 May 1993. Koto *Big Issue* 29 Mar 1994. FDA *St.Louis Post-Dispatch* 25 Dec 1984. Dentist *Guardian* 18 Dec 1979.

CHAPTER 9: IT'S A LOTTERY!

Dice *S.Mail* 11 Apr 1993, *D.Star* 28 Mar 1994. Raffles *Sun* 1 Mar 1988, *Sun* 14 Jul 1995. Roulette *S.Express* 17 Jul 1977. Wrong Lottery *The Globe* 17 Jun 1980. Porsche *Syllands Posten* 9 Jan 1991. Crime *S.Express* 20 Jan 1985, *Reuters* date unknown, *Nairobi Nation* 6 Nov 1990. Crossword *Observer* 6 Mar 1994. Dead *Today* 21 Nov 1992, *Arab News* 20 Aug 1988, *S.Mail* 7 Apr 1991. Texas *Edinburgh Eve. News* 14 Jan 1995. Thwarted *D.Record* 15 Aug 1994, *D.Record* 21 Feb 1994. Missed out *Int. Herald Tribune* 27 Apr 1995, *D.Express* 4 Jan 1978, *News of the World* 14 Jul

1991. Car Halifax Eve. Courier 14 Feb 1994, *Times of Malta* 17 Feb 1994. Thrown away *AP* 3 Dec 1994, *Standard* 15 May 1994. Garbage *Big Issue* 11 Jan 1994. Jilted *S.Express* 12 Mar 1995. Bus *Augusta Chronicle* 4 Jul 1994.

CHAPTER 10: DESTINY CALLING
Luck *D.Mirror* 11 Mar 1992. Careless *Metronews (Birmingham)* 4 Aug 1994, *D.Telegraph* 21 Sept 1988. Gobble *Winston-Salem Journal* 2 Jul 1993, *Western Morning News* 26 Feb 1993. Crook *Guardian* 10 Feb 1994, *D.Telegraph* 11 Nov 1988, *Wallasey News* 28 Mar 1980 Flood *Sun* 26 Oct 1992. Theatres *Glasgow Herald* 24 Feb 1992, *Edinburgh Eve. News* 6 Jun 1995. Chaos *D.Star* 13 Jul 1991, *Omaha World Herald* 19 Aug 1981. Sticks *Sun* 17 Dec 1991. Violent Storm *D.Mirror* 14 Mar 1992. Pine Falls *Sun* 27 Jan 1990, *Gwinnett D.News* 31 May 1990. Sloman *D.Telegraph* 20 Mar 1994, *D.Mail* 25 Sept 1981. Eel *Scunthorpe Eve. Telegraph* 24 Sept 1982. Blewitt *Scotsman* 18 Aug 1988. Nothing *Ashbury Park Press* 6 Jul 1988. Forletta *D.Telegraph* 7 Jun 1986, *D.Mirror* 18 Jun 1994.

CHAPTER 11: OOPS!
Plane *D.Star* 21 Dec. 1994. Sky-diver *Independent* 7 Apr 1988. Plane Pee *D.Telegraph* 23 Mar 1991. Thesis *New Scientist* 31 Jul 1993, *Western Mail* 9 Apr 1994. Photography *Weekly News* 23 Mar 1991, *The People* 4 Sept 1994, *D.Star* 20 Apr 1994. Lawyers *Eve. Post* 13 Jul 1988. Gum *The People* 5 Mar 1995. Milkman *Belfast Telegraph* 9 Mar 1994, *D.Record* 9 Nov 1995. Banner *D.Record* 4 Nov 1993. Butcher *Edinburgh Eve. News* 30 Jan 1992. Fire-eater *D.Star* 26 Apr 1994. Ball *D.Telegraph* 7 Feb 1995, *Correspondent* 9 Sept 1990. Wine *Sun* 26 Apr 1989. Gas *News of the World* 9 Jul 1995. Air Ads *Sussex Eve. Argus* 17 Sept 1993, *D.Mirror* 26 Oct 1993. Bald *D.Star* 16 Feb 1993. Honduran *Reuters* 1 May 1994. Brooch *D.Mirror* 7 Dec. 1993. Tin *D.Record* 11 Feb 1993.

CHAPTER 12: THE ROAD TO HELL
Food bags *D.Mirror* 26 Oct 1991. Apology *S.Express* 12 May 1991. Electricity *D.Record* 19 Feb 1991. Fish *Independent on Sunday* 25 Nov 1990. Sickness *S.Express* 11 Dec 1994, *D.Star* 17 Feb 1993. Fan *People* 27 May 1994. Beach *D.Telegraph* 28 Oct 1994. Muggers *Times* 9 Jul 1994. Bunny *D.Mirror* 22 Sept. 1981 Termites *San Jose Mercury News* 20 Jun 1992. Mosquitos *D.Mirror* 23 Sept 1987. Rat *D.Telegraph* 18 Feb 1994, *Today* 5 Aug. 1993. Police *D.Mail* 12 Jan 1995, *Guardian* 2 Aug 1995, Today 20 Feb 1993, *D.Star* 16 Feb 1993. Whale *New Scientist* 1 Apr 1995. Walkman *Southport, Ormskirk and Formby Star* 7 Oct 1992. Rings *D.Mirror* 11 Jul & 15 Oct 1992. Burns *St. Louis Jan Post-Dispatch* 9 Mar 1995. Samaritan *D.Telegraph* 27 Aug 1983. Paternity *The Times of Malta* 31 Jan 1994.

CHAPTER 13: SERVES 'EM RIGHT
Aliens *Times* 23 Mar 1993. Pigs *D.Star* 7 Jan 1995. Firework *San Jose Mercury News* 2 Jul 1993. Frying pan *D.Mirror* 9 Jun 1993. Lion *D.Express* 5 Nov 1988. Impersonation *Independent* 22 Jan 1993, *D.Record* 5 Nov 1994. Trees *Sun* 19 Dec 1990, *D.Star* 25 Feb 1994, *D.Star* 18 Jun 1993, *The People* 30 Oct. 1994. More Trees *Western D.Press* 1 Mar 1993. Rubber Plant *S.Wales Eve. Post* Aug 1992. Gliders *S.Express* 6 May 1990. Bomb *The People* 27 Nov 1994, *Sun* 19 Dec 1990. Grave *D.Telegraph* 12 Mar 1994. AIDS *The Lancet* 1991, *Guardian* 20 Jun 1995. Weld *The Courier Mail* 3 Jan 1992. Pig *Timosoara News* 7 Jan 1991, *Independent* 24 May 1991. Overeating *People* 20 Feb 1994, *Guardian* 26 Aug 1995.

CHAPTER 14: A BULLET WITH YOUR NAME ON

Rabbis *St. Louis Post-Despatch* 18 Mar 1992. Sex *Houston TX Chronicle* 14 Dec 1986, *Playboy* Aug 1982. Testicle *The Globe & Mail* 7 Feb 1983. Mayor *Guardian* 21 Feb 1985, *Toronto Globe & Mail* 21 Dec 1995. Dialysis *The Globe & Mail* 7 Feb 1983. Pen gun *D.Mirror* 27 Dec 1980. Unloading *D.Star* 12 Sept 1994, 21 Jul 1994. Animals *D.Express* 28 Oct 1978, Sun 31 Jul 1993. Asthma *Carbena Times* 28 Oct 1991. Toothache *Sussex Eve. Argus*. Mower *D.Record* 11 Apr 1994. Hammer *AP* 28 Dec 1995. Fortune-teller *The Sun* 13 Jan 1992, *D.Record* 19 Jul 1995. Suicide *D.Record* 18 Mar 1993, 14 Jan 1994. Depressed *S.Express* 5 Apr 1981. Marvo *Weekly World News* 9 Feb 1988. Elba *D.Express* 4 Jun 1982. Loo Paper *S.Express* 30 Nov 1980. Experts *News of the World* 15 Feb 1987. Imitators *Weekly News* 9 Feb 1985, *S.Express* 29 Feb 1976.

CHAPTER 15: I SPOKE TOO SOON

Bennett *D.Mirror* 7 Aug 1978. Jarlsson *The People* 17 September 1995. Klienberg *D.Star* 12 Jun 1990. School Bus *Augusta (GA) Chronicle-Herald* 5 Jun 1988. Parisian *S.Express* 6 Jan 1980. Flag *D.Mirror* 30 Sept 1987 Firefighters *New Philidelphia (OH) Times-Reporter* 23 Mar 1991. Hicks *D.Telegraph* 3 Sept 1993. Bog body *D.Mirror* 13 Dec 1983. Hold-up *S.Express* 4 Oct 1981. Molito *D.Record* 5 Dec 1992. Mortgage *S.Express* 13 December 1987. Teeth *Retail Newsagent* 18 Feb 1995. Meteorite *People* 16 Jan 1994. Cat *Expressen* 31 Aug 1995.

CHAPTER 16: WRONG END OF THE STICK

Ears *People* 19 Mar 1995. Flowers *D.Mirror* 19 Dec 1994. Bearded lady *S.Express* 11 Oct 1987, *Sun* 9 Jul 1992. Jealous wives *D.Record* 8 Nov 1993, *D.Record* 2 Oct 1992. Toddler *Arizona D.Star* 6 Dec 1994. Robber *Sunderland Echo* 19 Feb 1993. Solicitor *Europa Times* Dec 1993. Slaughterman *D.Star* 1 Dec 1994. Hedgehog *S.Mirror* 7 Aug 1994. Mohel *New York Post* 19 Oct 1993. Sausage *D.Mirror* 16 Apr 1992. Painkiller *D.Mirror* 16 Nov 1994. Coastguard *S.Mail* 1 Nov 1992. Log *Sun* 7 Mar 1992. Wrong Way *Bangkok Post* 29 Jun 1994. Fiagbe *Western Mail* 22 Jul 1994. Fake That *Aberdeen Press & Journal* Jun 1994. Carpet *People* 16 Jul 1995.

CHAPTER 17: STUCK!

Deckchair *Columbus Dispatch* 24 May 1989. Cement *Big Issue* 20-26 Mar 1995. Mud *Sussex Evening Argus* 19 Apr 1994. Callbox *Manchester Metro News* 10 Jun 1994, *D.Mirror* 10 Aug 1993. Condom *D.Telegraph* 16 Nov 1993. Vending machines *Guardian* 11 Jan 1995, *D.Mail* 13 May 1995. Toilets *Sheffield Star* 15 Sept 1995, *D.Telegraph* 29 Mar 1989, *Guardian* 16 Feb 1993. Snow *Santa Cruz Sentinel* 3 Jun 1995. Red Light *People* 31 Oct 1993. Revolving doors *D.Star* 29 Jan 1995. Lift *Yorkshire Post* 22 December 1995, *Rotherham Weekend Telegraph* 7 Jan 1995. Handcuffs *The Sun* 19 Feb 1994. Sauna *Today* 21 May 1990. Grave *The Guardian* 27 Aug 1993.

CHAPTER 18: SURPRISE!

Lightning *Sun* 24 Jul 1992, *Europa Times* Jan 1994. Dishwasher *Chicago Maroon* 20 Oct 1992, *New York Times* 8 Sept 1992. Loos *D.Mirror* 3 Jun 1995, *Bangkok Post* 30 Jul 1994. Wrong country *Clwyd & Chester Eve. Leader* 12 Jul 1993, *D.Telegraph* 1 Sept 1992. Poll tax *D.Mail* 16 Jan 1993. Yellow lines *Sussex Eve. Argus* 5 Apr 1994, *Kent Messenger Extra* 29 Sept 1995. Past *D.Mirror* 31 May 1990. Loving couples

Reuters 15 December 1995. Police *Sun* 2 Dec 1993, *San Jose Mercury* Jan 1993. Beacon *Weekly News* 8 Oct 1994. Scud *S.Mirror* 14 Apr 1991. Cow *Columbus Dispatch* 17 Sept 1990.

CHAPTER 19: HELL ON WHEELS

Golf Buggy *Big Issue* 17-23 Apr 1995. Beach Buggy *D.Star* 29 Apr 1994. Roofrack *D.Mirror* 5 Feb 1985. Opel *D.Mail* 4 Apr 1994. Own car *Edin. Eve. News* 21 Feb 1991, *D.Record* 22 Aug 1994. Ten times *D.Mirror* 25 Jun 1987. Boat *Sun* 28 Jun 1989. Yodellers *D.Mirror* 29 Jun 1994, *Coventry Eve. Telegraph* 30 Sept 1993. Antelope *Ivoir'Soir* 29 Dec 1994. Lobsters *D.News* 6 Nov 1993. Caravan *Independent* 24 Dec 1994. Wheels *D.Mirror* 11 Mar 1984. Temp *New York Post* 13 Oct 1993, *San Jose Mercury News* 14 Apr 1995. KGB *D.Star* 15 Mar 1993. Police bus *D.Mail* 28 Jun 1993. Schoolteacher *D.Telegraph* 15 Feb 1985, *S.Express* 3 Feb 1985, *Birmingham Eve. Mail* 1 Sept 1994.